The History of Horse Racing

FIRST PAST THE POST

Yum!

The History of Horse Racing

Champion thoroughbreds, owners, trainers and jockeys, illustrated with 220 drawings, paintings and photographs

John Carter

LORENZ BOOKS

This edition is published by Lorenz Books
an imprint of Anness Publishing Ltd
Blaby Road, Wigston, Leicestershire LE18 4SE
info@anness.com

www.lorenzbooks.com
www.annesspublishing.com

A CIP catalogue record for this book is available from the British Library.

Publisher: Joanna Lorenz
Production Manager: Steve Lang

Produced for Anness Publishing Ltd by
Editorial Developments, Edgmond,
Shropshire TF10 8JL, UK
Design: Bacroom Design and Advertising
Index: Marie Lorimer Indexing Services

PUBLISHER'S NOTE

Although the advice and information in this book are believed to be accurate and true at the time of going to press, neither the authors nor the publisher can accept any legal responsibility or liability for any errors or omissions that may have been made nor for any inaccuracies nor for any loss, harm or injury that comes about from following instructions or advice in this book.

Contents

***Right:** The sun sets over the statue of a racehorse at the entrance to Newmarket racecourse, England.*

Introduction

In October 2008, I spent a day in the English town of Newmarket, which proved to be an illuminating, almost surreal, experience for someone who was in the last throes of completing a work on the history of horse racing.

The town enlivened the words still milling around in my head because more than any other location on the planet, it contains both the history and heritage of the sport, as well as being a vibrant, modern-day headquarters.

You know you are in a racing town from the moment that the traffic lights turn red to allow a string of thoroughbreds to cross the road ahead on their way to dawn gallops. Those gallops represent the heart and soul of the town. It was here, some four centuries ago, that James I decided that the heathland would be ideal for his racing pursuits. It was here, too, that Charles II would perch in a chair at the top of Warren Hill and watch the horses take their morning exercise. Yet those gallops are used by three thousand thoroughbreds each morning in the twenty-first century, so it is far from a museum.

Equally, a walk through the town takes you past the historic offices of the Jockey Club, with the statue of little Hyperion who won the Epsom Derby in 1933. However, there are also numerous stables and studs, as well as two top quality racecourses, so the ancient merges seamlessly with the more contemporary.

Even at the Rowley Mile racecourse – the day I attended was Champions' Day, an autumnal showpiece that draws the curtain down on the English season – I passed by two ex-jockeys who have written their names large in the pantheon of the sport: Lester Piggott and Bob Champion. They were there to enjoy the occasion and watch modern icons: jockeys such as Frankie Dettori and thoroughbreds like New Approach who followed up his Epsom Derby win with a swan-song victory in the Champion Stakes, his last outing before he went to stud.

The town also hosts the bloodstock auctioneers, Tattersalls, first formed in 1766. A visit here acts as a reminder that the real stars of horse racing are, logically enough, thoroughbreds. They are a noble, athletic and attractive animal. While the sport owes much to its association with gambling and also provides money making opportunities and employment for many, the single most important factor in its ongoing popularity – at least it seems to me – is the relationship that man has with his horse.

Of course, the sport has spread its tentacles into many new and previously uncharted territories since Newmarket first hosted James I. Go to Australasia, go to the Americas, Africa or Asia and you will not need too much initiative to find yourself a race meeting to attend. Once there, part of the fun is that the basic principles are constant – horses running between two points in competition – but the flavour of the racing can be so charmingly different.

Truly, nowadays, it is a global phenomenon, with its elite performers, equine or human, always on the move in the search for the big prizes and the glory. Seven days after Newmarket's Champions' Day, many owners, trainers and jockeys were across the Atlantic for the Breeders' Cup in Santa Anita in California.

With this in mind there is an associated point worth making about this book. By the necessity of space it must focus on the elite performers who make the headlines. But in its many forms, at all levels, horse racing is a splendid, worldwide pastime, enjoyed by millions. It has a history rich with drama, sporting theatre and heroes, and, it is to be hoped, a future that will be just as successful.

Above: *Racehorses train on the gallops ahead of the first classics of the flat season at Newmarket, England.*

Below: *Horses jump out of the starting gates at the Breeders' Cup horse race at Belmont Park, USA.*

The Early Years of Horse Racing

Chapter 1: "This green plot shall be our stage"

Horse racing's exact birthplace and date has been the subject of much conjecture and debate yet has yielded little agreement among historians. It is known that horses were employed to pull chariots in warfare and Ben-Hur-like chariot races featured in the first Olympiad in 776 BC. There is also evidence that a form of racing took place during the Roman Empire in Britain around 200 AD, when two-horse challenges for private wagers seemed to be fashionable with nobility such as King Richard the Lionheart who was credited with issuing the first victory purse.

Other historians point to race meetings during the twelfth century at a horse fair in London and on Shrove Tuesday, both in London and at Chester – and certainly there is little doubt that by the sixteenth century racing was taking place at Doncaster, Carlisle and Chester. Indeed, it was at the latter location that a small wooden ball decorated with flowers was presented to the winner of a race in 1512. It was the first recorded evidence of a prize.

Below: *Historians differ on the origins of horse racing but all would agree that Town Moor at Doncaster, England, was one of the earliest 'green plots' to stage horse racing. Note the towering grandstand, started in 1776, for which the architect, John Carr, was paid 100 guineas.*

***Above:** A match race on the heathland at Newmarket circa 1720, between Grey Windham (owned by the Duke of Somerset) and Bay Bolton (Duke of Bolton). The sport gained momentum when it found itself a spiritual home here, largely thanks to a foggy night in 1603.*

So, one way or another, fertile seeds were being sown from which the kind of professional sport that is now enjoyed across the globe began to grow – and at the start of the seventeenth century, horse racing moved from trot to canter when it found itself a spiritual home. Serendipity was involved, with a fortuitous meeting of place, person and circumstance when James I arrived in the English town of Newmarket in 1603. He was forced by fog to stay overnight and, come the bright new dawn, recognized that the heathland was ideal for his hobby of racing horses. As a result, Newmarket came to see a great deal of the monarch. It became, and remains, a working town – inhabited by trainers, jockeys, stable lads, farriers and the like – with the racehorse at its core. Nowadays the flat expanses of heathland are populated by three thousand thoroughbreds each morning, partaking of their daily exercise.

***Right:** Another match race on the heathland, around 1684, this time between Charles II and Henry Jermyn. Even in the twenty-first century, Newmarket remains a town with horses and horse racing at its core.*

***Left*:**: *The famous Downs at Epsom have hosted top class horse racing for hundreds of years. The first recorded race took place here in 1661.*

Not long after Newmarket was inked in on the horse racing map it was joined by Epsom. The discovery of a small spring in the early seventeenth century saw it become a trendy and well-frequented spa town, the well-to-do seduced by the healthy properties of the water. Races on the Downs became part of the social scene, confirmation of which could be found in a burial document which stated, rather morbidly, that "William Stanley who is running the race fell from his horse and braik his neck". In addition Samuel Pepys recorded that there were "horsemen upon the hill where they were making matches to run". The first recorded race here took place in 1661, by 1684 it had its own clerk of the course and by 1730 there were regular meetings each spring and autumn.

Well before then, 'public' races had sprung up all over England with many of the events held at 'Bell Courses', so called because the prize was usually a silver bell. Royalty's interest continued to boost the sport's appeal. Charles I inherited James I's zest for riding and hunting and Charles II stayed in Newmarket for weeks at a time, accompanied by an entourage intent on disorderly pleasure. He used to sit perched at the top of the gallops in a little wooden kiosk known as 'The King's Chair' and observe the horses at exercise. Little wonder that horse racing became worthy of the label 'the sport of kings'. New York's colonial governor, Colonel Richard Nicholls, was another who visited Newmarket. He liked what he saw and returned home to build a racecourse in Long Island, New York, suitably named 'Newmarket' in homage. British settlers had already brought horses and horse racing to America but thanks to Nicholls's efforts its first formal race meeting was held in 1665.

Meanwhile, back in Britain, Queen Anne was another with blue blood who had a penchant for horses. She owned a large string and was instrumental in the founding of a racecourse at Ascot. Driving to Windsor Castle through Windsor Forest she came upon heathland that she saw as an ideal spot for racing. She bought the land and the first race was held in 1711. The right handed, triangular track is one that has stood the test of time, perhaps because there are few undulations, and it is recognized as a fair and true test of a horse's ability. The week of Royal Ascot has become one of the highlights of Britain's social scene as well as a race meeting of the highest class.

Below: *The sport of kings in a right royal setting in the early nineteenth century. The Royal Stand at Ascot hosts King George IV and his brother, Prince Frederick, Duke of York and Albany.*

Initially most racing was over the flat. However, in the middle of the eighteenth century, 'over the sticks' steeplechasing began to be popular in Ireland. Early, two horse contests, known as 'pounding races', involved cross-country slogs, jumping whatever obstacles the landscape threw in the way of horse and rider. The first recorded race took place over four a half miles between the towns of Buttevant and Doneraile in 1752. The start and finish were marked by the church steeple in each town, hence the term 'steeplechase'.

In William Shakespeare's *A Midsummer Night's Dream* there is a sentence of dialogue when Quince finds a suitable patch of land and exclaims "This green plot shall be our stage". It was around Shakespeare's time that the earliest 'green plots' at Doncaster and Newmarket in England first became established as a 'stage' for sport. It is clear that they were inspired choices. The greater the stage, the greater the theatre – and they have survived and prospered for several centuries.

Right: *From its beginnings in the eighteenth century, steeplechasing became increasingly popular. This is a scene from the 1839 Grand National at Aintree in England.*

Chapter 2: A Breed Apart

It is impossible to fully understand horse racing without understanding the importance of breeding in its development. The thoroughbreds currently followed on racetracks all around the globe are the product of four centuries, if not more, of selective breeding that has created a hybrid of its original form.

Left: *The Godolphin Arabian, painted by John Wootton. Foaled in 1724, he was one of three foundation stallions, forefathers of the modern-day thoroughbreds.*

The subject is incredibly complex and has endless subtleties, but, in essence, stallions who have been successful on the racetrack are matched with suitable mares. In that way it is intended that the species should evolve and develop. The aim is to create a kind of genetic harmony of physique and temperament because breeders and, in turn, owners crave thoroughbreds that yield prize money and so create a stud value for the future. Thus the cycle continues – with champion horses passing on their genes to future generations.

This pursuit can be profitable for breeders and owners, which is why flat racing's stars often have brief careers on the turf before retiring to stud, where their earnings can increase. The fact that a racehorse should be a 'Thoroughbred' is not merely preferable. It is a

Above: *The Byerly Turk, who was ridden by Captain Robert Byerly at the Battle of the Boyne in 1690. Another of the foundation stallions and, again, expertly painted by John Wootton.*

fundamental pre-requisite. For flat racing – as opposed to steeplechases where the male horses have usually been gelded and so cannot be used for breeding at the end of their careers – the pedigree of a horse is one of the requirements that permit it to compete. It must have a sire (father) and a dam (mother) who are purebred.

The Arabs were the first to employ selective breeding to produce better horses and, as early as the twelfth century, some turned up in England as knights returned from crusades with horses appropriated from Arab lands. By the sixteenth century, the horse used most frequently for racing in the British Isles was the 'hobby', a diminutive and durable species that had been originally imported from Spain to Ireland. They were well suited to the long-distance 'match races' which were usually contested by older horses.

At that stage the requirement was for thoroughbreds that could run long and often, but that has changed down the centuries. With an increasing desire to add speed to durability, early in the sixteenth century, Henry VIII imported a large number of Arabian stallions for breeding with British mares, resulting in the forefathers of the thoroughbreds racing today. Indeed, all modern racehorses descend in the male line from three foundation stallions: the Godolphin Arabian, the Byerly Turk and the Darley Arabian.

The Godolphin Arabian was the last born and least influential of the three. Foaled in 1724, he stood fourteen hands, three inches. He was allegedly a present to King Louis XIV of France from the Emperor of Morocco, before ultimately becoming the property of Lord Godolphin. Man o' War was one well-known descendant.

Above: *A beautiful early illustration depicting the popular sport of horse racing.*

Above: *The Darley Arabian, arguably the most influential of the venerated trio. Flying Childers and Eclipse were two notable descendants.*

Captain Robert Byerly rode the Byerly Turk, foaled in 1680, at the Battle of the Boyne in 1690, and the horse's fleetness of foot helped him avoid capture by opposition troops.

The Darley Arabian, foaled in 1700, was bought in Aleppo in 1704 for Mr. James Darley by his son, and has become the most influential of the three.

These three founding stallions all tended to 'stamp their stock', producing offspring that inherited their qualities along with those of the mare. Yet, in truth, breeding has always been a frustrating and imprecise science. As Derby winner trainer, Lieutenant Colonel Giles Loder, once said, "The only certainty in thoroughbred horse breeding is the uncertainty." So each new, little, uncoordinated foal had an invisible question mark hovering above its head. Regardless of its pedigree and purchase cost it could be a heart-breaking, money-losing letdown – or fulfil its owner's dreams and become a champion.

Of course, most fall somewhere in between, but, just occasionally, mould breakers like Flying Childers and Eclipse – both descendants of the Darley Arabian – became not just outstanding racehorses but actually represented a quantum leap forward in the evolution of the thoroughbred. Both were equine thunderbolts with dynamite in their hooves and wings on their backs.

Reports suggested that Flying Childers could cover twenty-five feet in a single stride and once sped across three and half miles in six minutes, forty seconds. He was described as "The fleetest horse that ever ran at Newmarket, or, as generally believed, that was ever bred in the world".

Right: *Flying Childers: "the fleetest horse that ever ran at Newmarket, or, as generally believed, that was ever bred in the world".*

Below: The 'wonderhorse' Eclipse: never headed, let alone beaten. The phrase "Eclipse first, the rest nowhere" has become part of racing vernacular as a result of his dominance.

His owner was the Duke of Devonshire, who turned down many offers for the colt, including one to pay for the horse's weight in gold. The exact number of races in which he competed is uncertain, but historians agree that he never came close to being beaten. When he retired to stud, he sired nearly five hundred winners until his death in 1741 at the age of twenty-six.

Eclipse, born twenty-five years later, was the great-great-grandson of the Darley Arabian and was named after the eclipse of the sun in the year of his birth. He was not raced until he was a mature five-year-old; legend states that he ran a trial race at Epsom and was spotted "running at a monstrous rate …the other horses would never catch him if he ran to the world's end". He won that first race and seventeen others, despite having been spared the whip and the spur. Not once was he headed, let alone beaten; albeit seven of the victories were walkovers because other owners simply declined to compete against him. He was just so much better than the rest. Indeed, the phrase "Eclipse first, the rest nowhere" has become proverbial.

Eclipse was a powerhouse, tall for his era at fifteen hands, three inches, with a massive heart (not uncommon down the years amongst horse racing's high performers) that weighed fourteen pounds, housed within a tall, elegant frame. He went to stud in 1771 and sired more than eight hundred and sixty winners.

However, despite the exploits of Flying Childers and Eclipse, it would be misleading to state that the quest to create excellence in racehorses was dominated by Great Britain. In 1673 Ireland's moderate climate was recognized as being perfect for breeding. "The soil is of sweet and plentiful grass", said Sir William Temple, "which will raise a large breed; and the hills, especially near the seacoasts, are hard and rough and so fit to give them shape and breadth and sound feet". Sure enough a large and prosperous bloodstock industry developed there. The same could be said for the United States of America, with Kentucky emerging as the bloodstock headquarters, again thanks to its clement weather, fertile soil and undulating geography. But Kentucky was not alone. Other centres were based in California, Maryland, New York, Florida and Virginia.

It was to Virginia that an English stallion called Bull Rock was imported to begin the whole breeding cycle in 1730. Bull Rock was by Darley Arabian out of a daughter of Byerly Turk, and so was a son and grandson of the founding stallions. By the American War of Independence, one hundred stallions and seventy mares had travelled from England to America, including four of the Epsom Derby winners.

Below: *Leading bloodstock auctioneers, Tattersall's, in 1838, the brainchild of Richard Tattersall.*

Right: *The pride of the United States of America in the nineteenth century: Lexington; a great racehorse and a prolific stallion at stud, topping the sire list on fourteen consecutive occasions.*

Jumping on a few decades, probably the greatest stallion of early racing was an American horse, Lexington. Born in 1850, and eventually reaching fifteen hands, three inches, he began under the name of Darley and easily won his first two races before a new owner changed his name to Lexington. Although he only competed seven times (winning six) many of his races were gruelling four-mile events. He was known as the best racehorse of his day, but retired early, at the end of 1855, with a hereditary eyesight condition. Then, if anything, he was more successful still at stud, topping the sire list for no less than fourteen consecutive years.

As the trend – slowly over many years – moved towards shorter races, often contested by three-year-olds, so the big prizes at auction were paid for early developing sprinters. Accordingly the thoroughbred evolved further with features that encouraged extreme speed. Hence the pencil thin legs, gluteal muscles and elongated tendons, with less bone mass and more muscle mass. They also became taller. Nineteenth-century racehorses towered, on average, six inches above their early predecessors. And so it continued – a never-ending quest for stronger, quicker, sounder and taller. Moreover, just as inevitably, a money-spinning industry was created in its wake, of which one essential facet was the auctioning of racehorses.

To that end, three years before Eclipse went to stud, bloodstock auctioneers Tattersall's was founded. It was the brainchild of Richard Tattersall who had been the stud groom to the second Duke of Kingston. The first premises were near Hyde Park Corner in what was then the outskirts of London. Two rooms were reserved for members of the newly formed Jockey Club, and they became the rendezvous for sporting and betting men.

The business was moved to Knightsbridge in 1865, and one hundred years later to Park Paddocks, Newmarket where its modern grounds are spacious and opulent. It is only two minutes from the modern-day Newmarket town centre but within the grounds of 'Tatt's' there is a colonial feel of going back in time, with immaculately maintained lawns, raked gravel, plentiful fauna and well-constructed stables, paddocks, examination and sales rings. In 1988 it also began holding auctions at Old Fairyhouse in Ireland. It remains one of the main auctioneers of racehorses in the United Kingdom and the Republic of Ireland, but other nations also became involved in breeding, and the venues of modern day bloodstock auctions reflect this.

Above: *In the eighteenth century, wagers were struck by individuals, often on match races. In this chaotic scene, some are offering to 'lay' or take odds, others are gambling with them or making counter offers.*

Chapter 3: Laws and Lawmakers, Rogues and Vagabonds

As early as 1617 the Doncaster Corporation, which owned the racecourse in the town, ordered the grandstand to be pulled down and the races to cease because of brawls and riots. In its formative years the "sport of kings" was also the sport of bad behaviour and downright cheating. Charles Greville (1794–1865) felt compelled to write in his diary, "The sport of horse racing has a peculiar and irresistible charm for persons of unblemished probity. What a pity that it makes just as strong appeal to the riff raff of every town and city."

Racing certainly attracted a diverse demographic, from rich aristocrats to the commoners who subsisted upon their crumbs. Racedays saw pickpocketing, people selling their wares, cockerel fighting and other sideshows.

Indeed, the early forms of racing were only similar to its modern equivalent in the sense that horses were ridden by jockeys and raced against each other between one designated point and another. Racedays were exhilarating and well attended – but also chaotic, as on-course gambling (at least in Britain) encouraged malpractice. As a result, in 1740, the British Parliament introduced an act "to restrain and to prevent the excessive increase in horse racing". The sport needed help, and was ripe for legislation and structure.

Right: *The famous Maryland Jockey Club seen during the 1950s.*

In America, the first local Jockey Club had already been formed in 1732 in South Carolina, followed by the Maryland Jockey Club. However, the most significant advance for the administration of the sport was when the British Jockey Club was created in 1752, based in Newmarket. At first its role was purely to arrange matches and settle bets, but soon it tried to bring law, order and governance to the sport. It published the first set of rules in 1758, and their influence and regulation of racing spread far wider than just Newmarket, far wider even than just Great Britain.

Among the British Jockey Club's early innovations was the recording of the coloured racing silks of its members "for the greater convenience of distinguishing the horses in running, but also for the prevention of disputes arising from not knowing the colours worn by each rider." This kind of advance was emulated worldwide, and formed a helpful starting point as others created their own formal code of conduct.

Left: *Coloured racing silks have long brought colour and clarity to racing since being formally introduced by the Jockey Club.*

HISTORY IN THE MAKING

Nineteenth-century match races

In 1752, Edmund Blake and Cornelius O'Callaghan agreed a wager to ride against each other on horseback across the Irish countryside and over various obstacles from one church to another: the code of horse racing that became known as 'steeplechasing' had begun. On the flat as well, these head-to-head contests – 'match races' – were common, both in Great Britain and the United States of America. They often involved multiple heats, and if a horse lost by more than two hundred and forty yards he was judged to have been 'distanced' and disqualified from further heats in that match. This was to prevent jockeys giving beaten horses an easy ride to keep them fresh for subsequent heats. In some countries, the phrase of coming up to 'the distance; (around a furlong from the finish) is still used.

Match races were most prevalent up to the end of the eighteenth century but continued well into the 1800s. The American Racing Manual lists ninety-nine such contests between 1822 and 1899, though many others would not have been recorded – and either side of the Atlantic there are many examples of celebrated and fiercely contested 'match races'.

Often they were preceded by months of preparation and speculation. Rivalries were intense, none more so than when, in 1806, the result of a match race led to a duel involving Andrew Jackson, who went on to serve two terms as President of the United States. Jackson's horse beat one owned by Charles Dickinson by sixty yards in a rainstorm in Nashville, Tennessee. The match had already been postponed due to rumours of wrongdoing, and the outcome enraged already volatile tempers. It was agreed that the two would duel with pistols at twenty-four paces. Dickinson fired first and, according to reports, his shot either missed Jackson completely or inflicted a slight foot wound. Either way the future President was in sufficiently good health to shoot Dickinson through the intestines, and he died the following day.

Left: *Andrew Jackson, seventh President of the the United States of America. Politician, lover of horse racing and, eventually, useful with a pistol in his hand.*

Among other notable examples of match races, the first hurdle race, in Bristol, England, was run in three one-mile heats over five hurdles in 1821. Two years later, American Eclipse, representing the Northern States, beat Sir Henry, representing the Southern States, two-one in a best-of-three contest. And no less than seventy thousand spectators – including forty senators – attended the match race between Fashion and Boston in 1842 in New York.

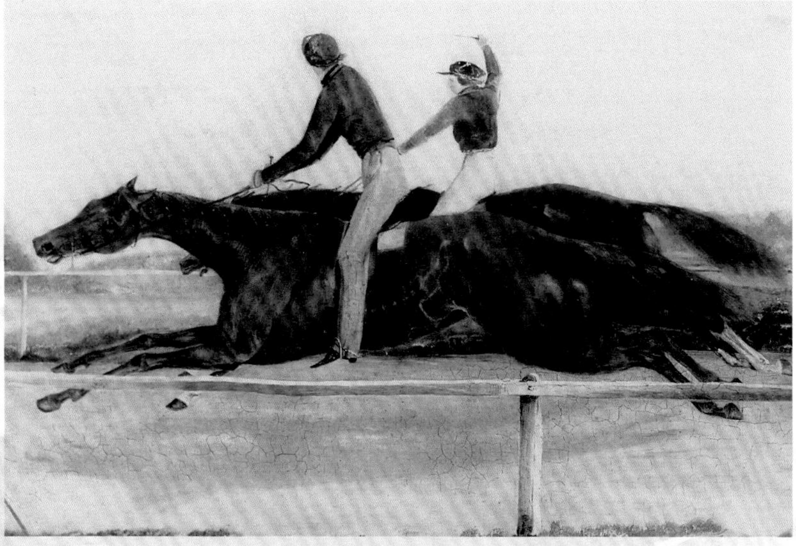

Above: *Fashion takes on Boston in front of seventy thousand spectators in New York. Fashion won.*

However, the contest that was dubbed the "match of the century" occurred when The Flying Dutchman defeated Voltigeur at York, England, in 1851. In 1849 The Flying Dutchman had won both the Derby and the St Leger; in 1850 Voltigeur repeated the trick. When the two double classic winners met in the Doncaster Cup, Voltigeur squeezed home by half a length, and the close-fought rivalry generated a re-match in May 1851 at York.

Both owners staked one thousand pounds, and Admiral Henry Rous's handicapping system determined that Voltigeur's extra age and previous victories would warrant a handicap of eight and a half pounds. The Flying Dutchman won by a short length in front of a vast crowd.

Right: *The "match of the century" contested by two classic winners. A magnificent spectacle as Flying Dutchman wins from Voltigeur in York, England.*

In 1828 the Australian Racing and Jockey Club was formed; in the 1830s the sport took hold in France with the French Jockey Club formed in 1863; and by 1866 The National Hunt Committee brought welcome regulation to a version of the sport that had fallen into decline.

As horse racing became more organized three administrators led the way; three good men and true, each a quintessential member of the English upper crust, each eager to shape the sport with their vision and dedication to reform.

The first was Sir Charles Bunbury, a model gentleman with a laid-back élan and a compassion towards horses that was several centuries ahead of his time. A contemporary once wrote, "He was a man naturally benign, of compassionate and friendly disposition and his plan for treating racehorses without suffering them to be abused by the whip and spur which he laboured so long and steadfastly, though unsuccessfully, to make general on the turf, ought ever to be remembered in his honour".

Bunbury became Steward of the Jockey Club in 1768 at the age of twenty-eight and moved in high society. Had he won the toss of a coin dining with Lord Derby, then what became the blue riband event of the English flat racing season would now be called 'The Bunbury Stakes' rather than 'The Derby Stakes' (refer to chapter four for further details). Indeed, all the English classics were founded in his time, contested by three-year-olds over distances between a mile and just over a mile and a half. He also oversaw the first recorded race between two-year-olds, all of which marked the beginning of the end for head-to-head 'match races' where one owner would challenge another, pitching two horses against each other over distances as long as four miles, sometimes in heats, with each side putting up a stake and the winner taking all.

Left: *Movers and shakers. The Governor's Box at Flemington Racecourse in Australia, around 1875. The gentlemen, from the left, are Sir George Bowers, Sir Hercules Robinson and Sir Anthony Musgrave.*

Below: *A cartoonist's impression of Sam Chifney and Escape, two pivotal figures in the conflict between the Prince of Wales (later George IV) and the Jockey Club's Sir Charles Bunbury.*

Advice regarding horses appeared as far back at 1616 when Gervase Marham's *Medicine for Horses* stated, "They are fit for the saddle at fore years of age, for the wars at six, for the race at eight, and for hunting or extreme matches, at ten or eleun". Certainly the competing horses in match races were usually mature and fully developed, with a need for stamina above speed.

Although it took another century for match races to fall entirely out of fashion, it was Bunbury who changed the emphasis. Under his stewardship the trend was clear: larger fields, younger horses, shorter distances – and this was entirely in keeping with his opposition to marathon slogs, which he felt put an undue strain on horses.

Bunbury may have displayed compassion towards the equine well-being but he was no soft touch as he demonstrated – albeit with limited success – when he locked horns with the then Prince of Wales, who later became George IV. During 1791 the Prince's colt, Escape, started favourite in a race and finished last of four. The next day he raced again and won easily, beating two of the horses who had previously beaten him. The illogical turnaround in fortunes became the subject of an investigation that pointed the finger of guilt at jockey, Sam Chifney.

Left: *Allez France! A vibrant scene at Longchamps Racecourse in 1864 for the second running of the Grand Prix, a year after the French Jockey Club had been formed.*

HISTORY IN THE MAKING

Epsom Downs, 1844

No single event better epitomized an era of intrigue and wrongdoing in horse racing than the 1844 Epsom Derby. Prior to the meeting a group of prominent racing figures, headed by Lord George Bentinck, had been suspicious of the activities of an owner, Goodman Levy, and believed that he was engineering a betting scam involving the swapping of two horses.

They sent a letter of protest to the Epsom stewards which stated that, in the opinion of the authors, the horse called Running Rein, due to take part in the race, was in fact four years old rather than the stipulated three and, indeed, was not actually the horse that his owner was purporting him to be. Of course, that extra year of physical maturity would gift the colt a considerable advantage over his opponents.

Left: *Derby Day on the Downs. A mix of characters and classes, it has always had a feel, a flavour, all of its own.*

To their disgust the stewards merely announced that they would investigate further should Running Rein win the race and permitted him to compete. To add to the drama and intrigue, during the race Running Rein collided with Leander, who broke his leg and had to be put down. Upon inspection, Leander was found to be a four-year-old, although his German owners later admitted that they believed he was actually six. The race's favourite was the victim of illegal riding and the second favourite was both 'nobbled' the night before and also 'pulled' by his jockey. That day Epsom was not so much a racecourse as a crime scene, and the spectators were misled.

Right: The 1844 running of the Derby is depicted; a remarkable race where all was not what it seemed.

Somewhat inevitably, Running Rein won by three-quarters of a length from Orlando. An appeal was immediately lodged and Lord Bentinck left no stone unturned in his quest for what he saw as justice. The case was heard in Westminster and it was confirmed that Bentinck and his associates had been right: the Derby winner had actually been a four-year-old called Maccabaeus, who had come under great suspicion the previous year when running as a supposed two-year-old at Newmarket. The race was awarded to the second-placed Orlando. The man who had engineered the deceit by switching horses, Goodman Levy, fled to France, and the Jockey Club publicly thanked Bentinck for this service to horse racing.

There have been many Derby days since – and no doubt some foul play – but surely the 1844 running of the race was a low point in terms of misdemeanour and deceit.

Right: The foot of the Downs between Tattenham Corner and the winning post.

Although nothing was ever proven, Bunbury informed the Prince that if he continued to employ Chifney on his horses he would have no one to race against. In short, the Jockey Club was decreeing that the heir to the throne would be disqualified from racing if he did not sever his links. However, the Prince would not be swayed and remained loyal to Chifney. Indeed the only links he severed were the ones with racing itself. He withdrew as an owner for fifteen years, though he continued to pay the jockey a retainer of two hundred guineas a year.

One of Bunbury's successors, Lord George Bentinck, was the third son of the fourth duke of Portland. He owned vast amounts of Newmarket Heath and became an influential member of the Jockey Club from 1802 – at a time when the nature of racing had changed, and not for the better.

Initially ownership had been the preserve of the upper classes. Six lords, five sirs, three dukes, a major, a colonel and a prince, for instance, won the first twenty Derbys. But in the years after the end of the Napoleonic War, other owners, intent on misdeeds, became prevalent and for a time – in Britain at least – horse racing was at its most unsavoury as horses were nobbled and jockeys accepted backhanders. For example, between 1809 and 1811, four racehorses died and others became very sick after drinking water poisoned with arsenic from a trough on Newmarket Heath. Daniel Dawson, a tout who hid in bushes on the heath watching trials and reporting to bookmakers, was found guilty and hanged in front of fifteen thousand onlookers. The bookmakers behind the plots got away scot-free.

Below: *Lord George Bentinck's Elis before the start of the St Leger. Note the van to the left of the image. This represented a notable innovation in equine transportation.*

It was impossible for Bentinck to eliminate this kind of wrongdoing but he did innovate. He was prominent in introducing 'vanning', where horses were taken to race meetings in vans rather than on foot. Indeed, his own St Leger winner, Elis, was one of the first to travel to a racecourse in this comparatively luxurious manner. Bentinck also brought more structure to the start of races and allocated numbers to horses on the racecard to aid identification.

At this stage, following the ebb and flow of a race was nigh on impossible for casual observers. For a time jockeys wore no distinguishing colours, horses wore no distinguishing numbers, and many of the horses were not even named (it was only in 1913 that all horses aged three or more had to have a name before they were allowed to race). Perhaps to aid identification, as well as for their own enjoyment, after the start of the race (which had been begun by the starter's shout of GO! before Bentinck became involved) spectators often rode down the racetrack after the horses. There could be as many as a thousand people on horseback pursuing the field towards the finish. Little wonder that in Newmarket in 1802 a spectator fell, was trampled on and brought down the horse behind him, which died. It had been bedlam. Towards the middle of the century a starting flag was introduced and the cavalry charge of spectators was banned.

In addition, Bentinck outlawed the practice of the winning owner giving a present to the judge after a big race; created a system of different enclosures at racecourses; fined clerks of the course for the late start of races; scrutinized jockeys weighing in and out with increased vigilance; and began to introduce shelter and refreshments for spectators.

All in all Bentinck could point to ample evidence that he had moved horse racing forwards by the time he progressed into the world of politics in 1846. Regrettably, he died of a heart attack two years later.

The third of the three, Admiral Henry Rous, was the brother of the Earl of Stradbroke and was born in 1791. Having spent time in the Navy, he was elected to the Jockey Club at the age of thirty and became Steward in 1838. Rous worked out the first 'weight for age' scales and became the public handicapper, a task that he fulfilled with vitality and enthusiasm. He once described gambling as "a necessary adjunct to racing", but he tried to ensure that each punter had a run for their stake money.

Somewhat unconventionally, at his hometown course of Newmarket he would hide in the bushes around two furlongs from the finish and bellow at jockeys who he felt were not pushing their mounts sufficiently.

These three turf reformers – Bunbury, Bentinck and Rous – were undoubtedly forces for good, but it would be wrong to think of them as horse racing's saviours. The importance of gambling to the sport, and the wide range of racegoers that it attracted, encouraged misdeed – and certainly this continued to occur well beyond their terms of office.

The Duke of Omnium in Anthony Trollope's *The Duke's Children,* written in 1880, states: "Races! A congregation of all the worst blackguards in the county, mixed with the greatest fools!" In addition, South African owner, Sir Abe Bailey, said as recently as 1925, "I do not say that all who go to racing are rogues and vagabonds, but I do say that all the rogues and vagabonds seem to go to racing."

However, racing gradually became a cleaner sport and the contributions of the various Jockey Clubs were vital in helping horse racing to become a sustainable, regulated pastime, giving pleasure to millions.

Above: *Turf reformer and Jockey Club steward, Admiral Henry Rous was an innovator and handicapper, a task he fulfilled with a passionate energy.*

Below: *The first weight-for-age scale, created by Admiral Henry Rous. This proved an essential building block for effective handicapping.*

STANDARD WEIGHTS FOR AGE.

126 TABLE OF STANDARD

Age. Years.	April 1. st. lb.	May 1. st. lb.	June 1. st. lb.	July 1. st. lb.	Aug. 1. st. lb.	Sept. 1. st. lb.	Oct. 1. st. lb.	Nov. 1. st. lb.
HALF A MILE.								
2	5 2	5 7	5 12	6 1	6 3	6 5	6 7	6 8
3	7 5	7 7½	7 10	7 13	8 0	8 1	8 1½	8 2
4	8 7	8 7	8 7	8 7	8 7	8 7	8 7	8 7
5, 6, & a	8 9	8 8	8 7½	8 7	8 7	8 7	8 7	8 7
T. Y. C., OR SIX FURLONGS.								
2	4 9	4 13	5 3	5 6	5 8	5 10	5 12	6 0
3	7 2	7 4	7 6	7 7½	7 9	7 10	7 11	7 12
4	8 7	8 7	8 7	8 7	8 7	8 7	8 7	8 7
5, 6, & a.	8 13	8 12	8 11¼	8 11	8 10½	8 10	8 9	8 8
ONE MILE.								
2	4 2	4 7	4 12	5 0	5 2	5 3	5 4	5 5
3	6 12	6 13	7 1	7 4	7 6	7 7	7 8	7 9
4	8 7	8 7	8 7	8 7	8 7	8 7	8 7	8 7
5	9 0	8 13¼	8 13	8 12½	8 12	8 11¼	8 11	8 10
6 & aged	9 1	9 0	8 13½	8 13	8 12	8 11½	8 11	8 10

Champions and Champion Jockeys

Chapter 4: Blue Ribands

During the eighteenth and nineteenth centuries more 'green plots' of land became the stage for horse racing, and, in addition, the calendar became punctuated with 'blue riband' occasions, many of which still remain.

At the end of the eighteenth century and the beginning of the next, the set of five English 'classic' races came into being. Of course it is only with the benefit of hindsight that we can label them in this way. At the time they were just a series of innovations – with one of racing's great administrators, Sir Charles Bunbury, to the fore – that took root. During the early years the attention of the British public was with the Napoleonic Wars and there was little newspaper coverage. It was not until the 1880s that the five races were packaged together and known as the 'classics'. However, by then their stature and the prize money attracted horses, trainers and jockeys like moths to the flame.

Certainly the races have stood the test of time. The oldest of them has now lasted more than two hundred and thirty years – and for that we must thank Colonel Anthony St Leger who initiated the first St Leger in 1776, run over two miles at Cantley Common, close to the current location for the race, Town Moor in Doncaster.

By then the racecourse was already hosting the 'Doncaster Cup', first contested in 1766 over two and a quarter miles. However, the St Leger achieved the greater fame. Like all the English classics, it is purely for three-year-olds – and was run over one mile, six furlongs and one hundred and thirty-two yards. In addition to being the longest in distance, the St Leger became, chronologically, the final classic of each season.

Below: *The St Leger, oldest of the English classics. First contested in 1776, this is the 1836 running, won by Elis, owned by Lord George Bentinck.*

Three years after the birth of the St Leger the first Oaks was run, courtesy of the Twelfth Earl of Derby, who had decided, the previous year, to introduce a race for fillies over one and a half miles. The race was named after the country house that he had leased a few years earlier and was run on the Downs at Epsom.

During the celebration after the first Oaks, the Earl, whose horse had been victorious in the race, was inspired by conversations with Sir Charles Bunbury, to introduce an additional race. But what to call it? To decide they agreed to toss a coin and name the race after the winner. It was the Earl who won and 'The Derby' came into existence.

It must have been some compensation for Bunbury that his horse, Diomed, claimed victory in the inaugural running, collecting prize money of one thousand and sixty-five guineas. The first four runnings of the race were over a distance of one mile but this was amended in 1784 to the current distance of one mile and four furlongs.

Above: *Sir Charles Bunbury's Diomed, winner of the first Epsom Derby. This was some consolation for Bunbury. If the toss of a coin had fallen in his favour the race would have been named in his honour.*

Above: *A cigarette card of the period depicting the Melbourne Cup, Australia, in 1928.*

In 1851 Charles Dickens wrote that "On Derby Day a population rolls and scrambles through the place that may be counted in millions". Certainly race days were coloured by a large and diverse microcosm of society; diversity, incidentally, that was also displayed – and is still displayed – at equivalent events around the world such as Australia's Melbourne Cup and America's Kentucky Derby.

In the early days at Epsom, beggars, gypsies, tricksters, acrobats, and salesmen greeted the rich and prosperous. They are less seen nowadays but there is still a clear distinction between those in their fine dresses, top hats and morning suits, eating lobster and drinking champagne, and those who inhabit the hill on the inside of the racetrack, enjoying a more informal party atmosphere.

The Derby has always been an eclectic and quirky occasion; and the quirkiness extends to the racetrack. The present, rollercoaster Derby course has been used since 1872. The first half mile rises for one hundred and fifty feet, before plunging back downhill for one hundred feet. The field then takes a sharp left-handed turn into the finishing straight with a disorienting camber.

Below: *The Kentucky Derby, 1934 – America's equivalent of the Epsom Derby and the Melbourne Cup.*

Equine all-rounders have tended to prosper at the Derby. Winners need speed to take up a good position in the hectic early stages and, later, kick for home; agility and balance to handle the slopes, Tattenham Corner and the camber on the home straight; and stamina, fortitude and persistence to continue with the lung-bursting effort through the final furlongs.

Visiting Australian jockey Mick Goreham, who rode in the 1974 Derby, said, "It's the queerest course I've ever ridden on. It is not just the hill but also the angle. I never expected to see anything like that. And to think you run the greatest race in the world on it. I feel most trainers would take one look at it and put their horses right back in the box".

Despite its quirkiness – perhaps because of it – Epsom's Derby became, and remains, the most prestigious flat racing event in Britain. It is now part of a nation's heritage.

In view of its role as the spiritual home of British horse racing, it was appropriate that Newmarket should complete the set and host the fourth and fifth classics. They were the One Thousand and Two Thousand Guineas.

The name of the Two Thousand Guineas derived from its first event when there were twenty-three entries, all contributing one hundred guineas each. This was rounded down and hence the name for this one-mile race for three-year-old colts and fillies.

Five years later, in 1814, a race was run between ten fillies that, again, were entered at a subscription of one hundred guineas each, leading to the name of the One Thousand Guineas.

Above right: *The field rounds Tattenham Corner on Epsom's Derby Day in 1955. The severity of the turn and the camber of the turf provide a challenge to horse and rider.*

Right: *Sceptre, who won not only the One Thousand and Two Thousand Guineas in 1902, but all of the English classics with the exception of the Derby where she finished fourth. A remarkable tour de force.*

Thus, early in the nineteenth century, the English 'classics' were all up and running: the One Thousand and Two Thousand Guineas in Newmarket in May; the Oaks and the Derby at Epsom in June and the St Leger at Doncaster in September.

By then Ascot could boast its own feature race, the Gold Cup, which was first run in 1807 with the Prince Regent – whose father had commissioned the building of the permanent stand – among the spectators. And, year by year, racing mushroomed into new territories. A meeting was recorded in 1774 at Ayr in Scotland, and in 1804 the Ayr Gold Cup, run over the flat, was inaugurated.

In Ireland, too, seeds had long been sown. The Curragh – Ireland's equivalent of Newmarket – is the modern word for 'cuireach', Gaelic for racecourse. It is known that in the third century AD the current site hosted chariot races. Between 1817 and 1824 a race called the O'Darby Stakes (intended to become the Irish counterpart to Epsom's Derby) was introduced, followed by the Curragh Derby in 1848. Alas, both flopped, but in 1864 Lord Howth, the Marquis of Drogheda, and the Earl of Charlemont inaugurated the Irish Derby. Just three horses raced in the first event, and only two in the third year, but in 1907 an entry from the Epsom Derby winner, Orby, helped to give the race credibility and stature. Nowadays all the Irish classics are held at the Curragh.

Above: *The Irish Derby at the Curragh in 1995. All the Irish classics are held here.*

Left: *Flyon easily wins the 1939 Ascot Gold Cup. Ascot became one the elite venues in British horse racing and the Royal Ascot meeting provides some of the highest quality horse racing in the world.*

The first use of the term 'steeplechase' on an official racecard was also in Ireland in the early nineteenth century. Organized steeplechasing in Britain began with annual, cross-country events over a number of fields, hedges and brooks, the most notable of these being the St Albans Steeplechase, first run in 1830.

Cheltenham is now synonymous with steeplechasing but, from 1819, the Cheltenham Gold Cup was run over three miles of flat terrain. Cheltenham had chequered beginnings. At a time when horse racing was associated with dubious morals, the Evangelical Rev Francis Close preached on the sins of gambling at Cheltenham; in 1829 there was a course demonstration; and a year later the grandstand burned down. Racing here stopped and did not start again until the turn of the century, and it then moved to the current site where it has enjoyed a smoother history.

Below: *Horses and riders tumble at Becher's Brook at Aintree, 1959.*

HISTORY IN THE MAKING

Newmarket, England, 1886

By the age of twenty-nine, in 1886, the jockey Fred Archer had become venerated by the English public. Though pencil slim, pallid in complexion and buck-toothed, he had gained folk-hero status.

Archer was born near the site of the Cheltenham racecourse in 1857 and became an apprentice jockey with the trainer Matthew Dawson at the age of eleven, gaining respect from both Dawson and all involved at the yard for his ability to ride fearlessly the more difficult horses. He was the stable jockey with Dawson between 1874 and 1886, and they made such a winning partnership that Archer was champion for thirteen consecutive years until 1886, riding two thousand, seven hundred and forty-eight winners from eight thousand and eighty-four starts. He won a total of twenty-one classic races, including the Epsom Derby five times.

Nerves of iron, capability and an all-consuming, compulsive yearning to win fuelled the impressive statistics, as is often the case with high-achieving sportsmen. Before races Archer would examine the opposition in detail, and he took defeat to heart. Nor was he above taking the necessary opportunist steps to secure the best rides. And then, quite suddenly and wretchedly, with his career still in the ascendancy, the supreme jockey of the Victorian era was dead.

Some said that the appalling 'wasting' – starvation might be a more accurate word – caused it. Jockeys were so indebted to trainers that they would 'waste' in what we would now see as a dangerous way, depriving themselves of nutrients, calories and hydration so they could reduce the weight on a horse's back and encourage trainers to employ their services. Archer's self-imposed regime was, out of what he saw as professional necessity, absolutely brutal.

Right: *A master craftsman at work. The foremost jockey of the Victorian era, Fred Archer, rides Ormonde.*

When he had won his first race at the age of twelve he weighed just four stone eleven pounds, but he grew to five foot eight and a half inches – very tall for a jockey, particularly in the Victoria era. As a result his career became an ongoing, irreconcilable conflict between his talent and the length of his frame. He had to fast more than other jockeys. To help, he drank a purgative known as 'Archer's Mixture' that was so concentrated that a friend was unable to go racing the next day after he had sampled a spoonful. In short, few doubted that the 'wasting' had a long-term impact on his health and his psychological well-being.

***Far right:** Fred Archer at ease on board Bendor. Away from the saddle and the racetrack, he was less comfortable.*

***Right:** A fashionable check suit for a national icon.*

Others pointed to the recent death of his wife, Nellie Rose, in childbirth and the fact that their son, William, had also died prematurely – and some noted that he had been suffering from a high fever and delirium caused by typhus.

Whatever the reasons, on 8th November 1886, horse racing's biggest star took his own life with a single shot to the head from a pistol. Unbalanced, his muddled mind could take no more. The tragic news prompted a remarkable outpouring of public grief. On the day the news broke, buses in London stopped every few yards so that people could buy an evening paper. The Prince of Wales sent a wreath to the funeral, and Archer's hometown of Newmarket came to a standstill on the day that he was buried alongside his wife and son. Their combined ages totalled just fifty-two years. Since that sad day there have been many reported sightings of Archer's ghost.

Fred Archer: champion jockey, public favourite; a career, a life, prematurely ended.

Below: *The 1839 Grand National, depicted by Charles Hunt. The race attracted huge crowds from the outset.*

However, the future prosperity of steeplechasing was guaranteed by the addition of a new race. Some additions to the racing calendar have been slow burners, with their eminence growing over the years. Others, such as the Grand National, immediately caught racegoers' imagination. Run at the Aintree racecourse on the outskirts of Liverpool, it was founded by hotel owner William Lynn and was first run in 1839.

In the days leading up to the race, people flocked to Aintree by railway, steamer, coach, gig, wagon, on horseback and on foot. Reports from Liverpool hotels suggested that many slept four to a bed. Predictably the grandstand was bursting at the seams as seventeen horses attempted the four and a half mile endurance test. Conditions stated that "No rider was to open a gate or ride through a gateway, or more than one hundred yards along any road, footpath or driftway".

Many of the twenty-nine obstacles were small but others were more difficult, such as a five foot high stone wall in front of the grandstand. In addition there were two brooks. The first presented a formidable challenge: there was "a strong paling, next a rough, high jagged hedge and lastly a brook about six feet wide". Regrettably for one Captain Becher, his mount hit the paling at speed and Becher received an unwanted head-first dunking in the brook. Legend states that he later exclaimed that he had "never tasted water so foul without whisky in it," and the obstacle became known as 'Becher's Brook'. He remounted but his race was finally ended when he was deposited in water once more at what is now called 'Valentine's Brook'.

Above: *Landing sides – the challenge that awaits at Becher's Brook (inset) and Valentine's Brook (main) at the Aintree racecourse in England, home of the Grand National. Becher's Brook posed, and still poses, a particularly severe challenge for horse and rider as the landing area drops several feet compared with where they take off.*

The experience of Captain Becher told us much about the nature of the Grand National; an examination of fortitude and bravery – with gross good fortune also needed – for a cavalry charge of horses and jockeys. Each year brought new thrills and spills, heroes and hard luck stories. It was somehow appropriate that the first winner was named Lottery.

If the Grand National became a catalyst for the popularity of steeplechasing in Britain then the Melbourne Cup did much the same for horse racing in Australia. Interest had gathered momentum here through the nineteenth century. Twenty-two years after the first horses had arrived in Australia, the first official race meeting in the country took place in Sydney, New South Wales, in 1810. Other states gradually followed suit: Tasmania in 1814; Western Australia in 1833; South Australia in 1838; and Queensland in 1843. However, the country's racing headquarters – the equivalent to Newmarket and Kentucky, in Britain and America respectively – emerged as Victoria and, specifically, Melbourne.

Victoria's first meeting was held in 1838, and the first at the Flemington racecourse, seven kilometres west of Melbourne, was two years later. From 1855 Melbourne hosted the Victoria Derby but the continent found itself a flagship event to place Australian racing firmly on the map from 1861 with what was to become known as 'the world's greatest handicap'. It spanned three thousand and two hundred metres of Flemington's pear-shaped track and was contested by three-year-olds and over. The first Tuesday in November became the day that the nation stopped and turned its attention to picking the winner of the Melbourne Cup.

Below: *A painting of the inaugural Grand National in 1839.*

Below: *The bravery required – both by human and equine contestants – to compete in the Grand National is clear in this photograph of the race in 1928.*

__Right:__ A sociable scene from the paddock area at the Victorian Derby in 1886. The races attracted only slightly smaller crowds than the popular Melbourne Cup.

__Left:__ A crashing fall in 1996 at Aintree.

A crowd of four thousand (twenty years later it had ballooned to one hundred thousand) watched seventeen horses contesting the inaugural event in the quest for one hundred and seventy pounds and a gold watch. Some say that the first winner, Archer – the horse rather than the famous English jockey of the same name – was walked eight hundred kilometres to the course from New South Wales. Archer won again the following November, but because his owner's nomination form arrived late the next year, was prevented from going for the hat-trick. Sympathetic owners boycotted the race which, as a result, started with only seven horses, still the smallest field in its history. However, it just was a temporary setback and the event has continued to grow in magnitude.

"Sure, the Poms have Ascot and the Frogs have the Arc, and the Yanks their Kentucky Derby and Breeders Cup" said Australia's National Racehorse Owners' Association in 1995, "but nowhere in the world do they have such a grand racetrack party, which lasts a whole week and gives way to a true carnival cocktail of colour, culture, coiffure and couture." And they might just have a point. Certainly it encouraged the introduction of other high profile races in Australia such as the Caulfield Cup and the Stradbroke Handicap.

Above: *The Irish love their horse racing, either 'on the flat' or 'over the sticks'. Here Ross Geraghty wins the Irish Grand National on Bunny Boiler at Fairyhouse.*

Left: *A stylish, vibrant and sociable scene at the French home of horse racing, Longchamp, on the outskirts of Paris in 1870.*

Two years after Australia's flagship event began, France had an equivalent: 'Le Grand Prix de Paris'. In 1854 the French governing body authorized a racecourse to be built at Longchamp, in parkland to the west of Paris. The first meeting took place three years later with more than one hundred thousand in attendance, including the Emperor Louis Napoleon. Since then Longchamps has been the venue for the majority of France's big racedays and 'Le Grand Prix de Paris' – originally over two miles but reduced to ten furlongs – was introduced in 1863, swiftly becoming a highlight of the Parisian social calendar. It was not until October 1920 that Le Prix de l'Arc de Triomphe, the all age, middle distance championship of Europe began. Also on the outskirts of Paris is Auteuil, France's premier jumping track, which has held Le Grand Steeplechase de Paris since 1874. Meanwhile, Ireland's Fairyhouse racecourse, with its delightfully rural location, was introduced in 1860 and became the venue of the Irish Grand National.

Below: *The atmospheric spires of Churchill Downs in the background as Big Brown powers to victory in the 2008 running of the Kentucky Derby.*

HISTORY IN THE MAKING

Flemington, Australia, 1890

In 1890 Flemington racecourse celebrated its fiftieth birthday with a vibrant atmosphere for the Melbourne Cup. Certainly there was good cause for cheer because the race had become established in the horse racing calendar. In the Melbourne metropolitan area, raceday had been a public holiday since 1877 but all of Australia stopped – and still stops – on the first Tuesday of November for the Melbourne Cup.

There were a record thirty-nine starters in 1890 and one of them, a compact and stocky bay colt from New Zealand called Carbine, bore a record handicap of ten stone, five pounds. Because the race is a handicap, the weight to be carried is adjusted based on the horse's age and previous results – and in the case of the five-year-old Carbine, his previous results were highly impressive. He was unbeaten in five starts as a two-year-old in New Zealand before being transported to Australia where he won nine of thirteen starts as a three-year-old. One highlight was his win in the AJC Sydney Cup over two miles. Despite suffering interference at the half mile post that reduced him to last place in the running, Carbine stormed home to win by a head in a race record time. As a four- and five-year-old he won seventeen out of eighteen races.

***Left:** Carbine – a horse that became a legend.*

Despite carrying a burdensome weight on his back, the Australian punters displayed such loyalty to the horse nicknamed 'Old Jack', that he began the Melbourne Cup as a four to one favourite. They had been backing him for months, yet surely these odds overstated his chances. Surely the handicap would be too much. Eighty-five thousand were interested enough to turn up to watch.

When Carbine cantered onto the racetrack there was a burst of cheering so loud and enthusiastic that it 'spooked' him and he declined to go to the post, rooted to the spot. It required a hefty push from behind to get him moving and he then had to be dragged down the starting gate, appearing as though he would rather be anywhere on the planet. But once the race started he appeared more interested, holding a good position throughout. And once the large field hit the home straight his class began to tell, with the urging of his supporters rising ever louder as he motored forward, seemingly oblivious to the extra load. An opening emerged through the centre of the racetrack and Carbine eased through to win by two and a half lengths in a new race record time. He had carried fifty-three pounds more than the second placed horse, thirty-three to one outsider, Highborn. It was a remarkable demonstration and the reaction of the crowd was just as noteworthy. It was a jubilant scene of cheers and hurrahs.

***Left:** Spearmint, the 1906 Epsom Derby winner – one of Carbine's many successful progenies.*

The *Melbourne Punch* summed it up: "There was never a Melbourne Cup like Carbine's. Those who saw it are never likely to forget it. The tumult after his victory was unbelievable. The great horse stood, quivered a little and took the tumult as his due. Thus was a legend born, for he became a symbol of courage, the great hearted stayer who triumphed while carrying a punishing load."

At the end of his fifth season Carbine was retired to stud in Australia and then taken to England where he sired Spearmint, the 1906 Epsom Derby winner. And, down the line, two direct descendants, Old Rowley (1940) and Rainbird (1945), repeated their distant relation's glories at the Melbourne Cup.

***Left:** The Melbourne Cup, 1890. Carbine's finest hour as he made light of a heavy handicap to win in a record time.*

By then racing in the United States of America was established. George Washington, who later became its first President, attended several race meetings in Maryland between 1771 and 1773. By 1831 Kentucky had not only emerged as a centre for thoroughbred breeding but hosted the inaugural running of the Phoenix Stakes, the oldest stakes event still in existence in America.

In 1872, Colonel Meriwether Lewis Clark, Jr. had visited the Epsom Derby. Suitably inspired he returned home to Kentucky and organized the Louisville Jockey Club to raise money for facilities that funded the construction of the Churchill Downs racetrack, based on Epsom. It has subsequently become famous across the racing world for its trademark twin spires and the Kentucky Derby.

First the statistics: the Derby is contested on a dirt racetrack by three-year-old thoroughbreds, and is held annually on the first Saturday in May, capping the two-week-long Kentucky Derby Festival. On 17th May 1875, a field of fifteen contested the first Derby over one and a half miles; the same distance as the Epsom Derby and the Grand Prix de Paris. Twenty-one years later, the distance was changed to its current distance of one and a quarter miles.

However, cold figures cannot begin to convey the flavour of the occasion. Irwin S. Cobb said, "Until you go to Kentucky and with your own eyes behold the Derby, you ain't never been nowhere and you ain't seen nothing". In addition, John Steinbeck wrote, "The Kentucky Derby, whatever it is – a race, an emotion, turbulence, an explosion – is one of the most beautiful and satisfying things I ever experienced".

Right: *The 'Run for the Roses' reaches its climax – winner Big Brown in action in 2008.*

Above: *The taste of the Kentucky Derby – Mint Julep.*

In addition to the race itself, to 'get' the Kentucky Derby one needs to bombard the senses: drink the mint julep, taste the burgoo, listen to the marching bands and smell the roses. To explain: the mint julep is an iced drink consisting of bourbon, mint and sugar syrup which patrons often sip from a souvenir glass printed with all previous Derby winners. Burgoo, a thick stew of beef, chicken, pork and vegetables, is a popular Kentucky dish served at the Derby. As the horses are paraded before the grandstands, the University of Louisville marching band plays Stephen Foster's "My Old Kentucky Home". And a garland of five hundred and fifty-four red roses is placed around the winning horse's neck each year. This led to the race being nicknamed 'The Run for the Roses'.

Of course raceday crowds of around one hundred and fifty thousand also add to the sense of occasion as they celebrate spring's arrival, the gathering momentum of a new racing season and the first leg of the U.S. Triple Crown. As with the English Derby they are split; between the cream of society in the exclusive viewing areas – there to see and be seen – and the masses in the 'infield', where there is limited viewing but cheaper admission and a carnival atmosphere.

Below: *Top of the stretch at the Preakness Stakes at Pimlico – the second leg of the U.S. Triple Crown.*

The second leg of the Triple Crown is the Preakness Stakes, run at the Pimlico racecourse in Baltimore, Maryland. Pimlico was founded in 1870, the second oldest racecourse in the States, and the first Preakness Stakes was run three years later. It is contested by three-year-olds over a distance of one mile and one and a half furlongs, two weeks after the Kentucky Derby. Pimlico has traditions of its own, of which one is that the horse weathervane which stands in the winner's circle is painted the colour of the winning owner's silks immediately after the Preakness is completed.

The concluding and oldest jewel in the Triple Crown is the Belmont Stakes – named after August Belmont – which has been contested in several locations. It began life at Jerome Park, Westchester, New York, in 1867; moved to Morris Park in 1890; and moved again to Belmont Park, the largest and possibly plushest racecourse in the States, in 1905. Twenty miles out of New York it was constructed in the Jamaican district, at a cost of two and half million dollars. The race nowadays is over one and a half miles, testing the stamina and resolve of any Triple Crown aspirants. It is held on the third Saturday after the Preakness Stakes.

By the end of the nineteenth century the Kentucky Derby, the Preakness Stakes and the Belmont Stakes had become packaged together as 'The U.S. Triple Crown'.

So as horse racing moved into the twentieth century each racing season had a tempo to it, with annually held meetings and races creating an ebb and flow. Each one had its own flavour and, in time, its own heritage and history. Racegoers with imagination could appreciate that the latest batch of thoroughbreds racing before them were, almost literally, running in the hoof prints of champions past.

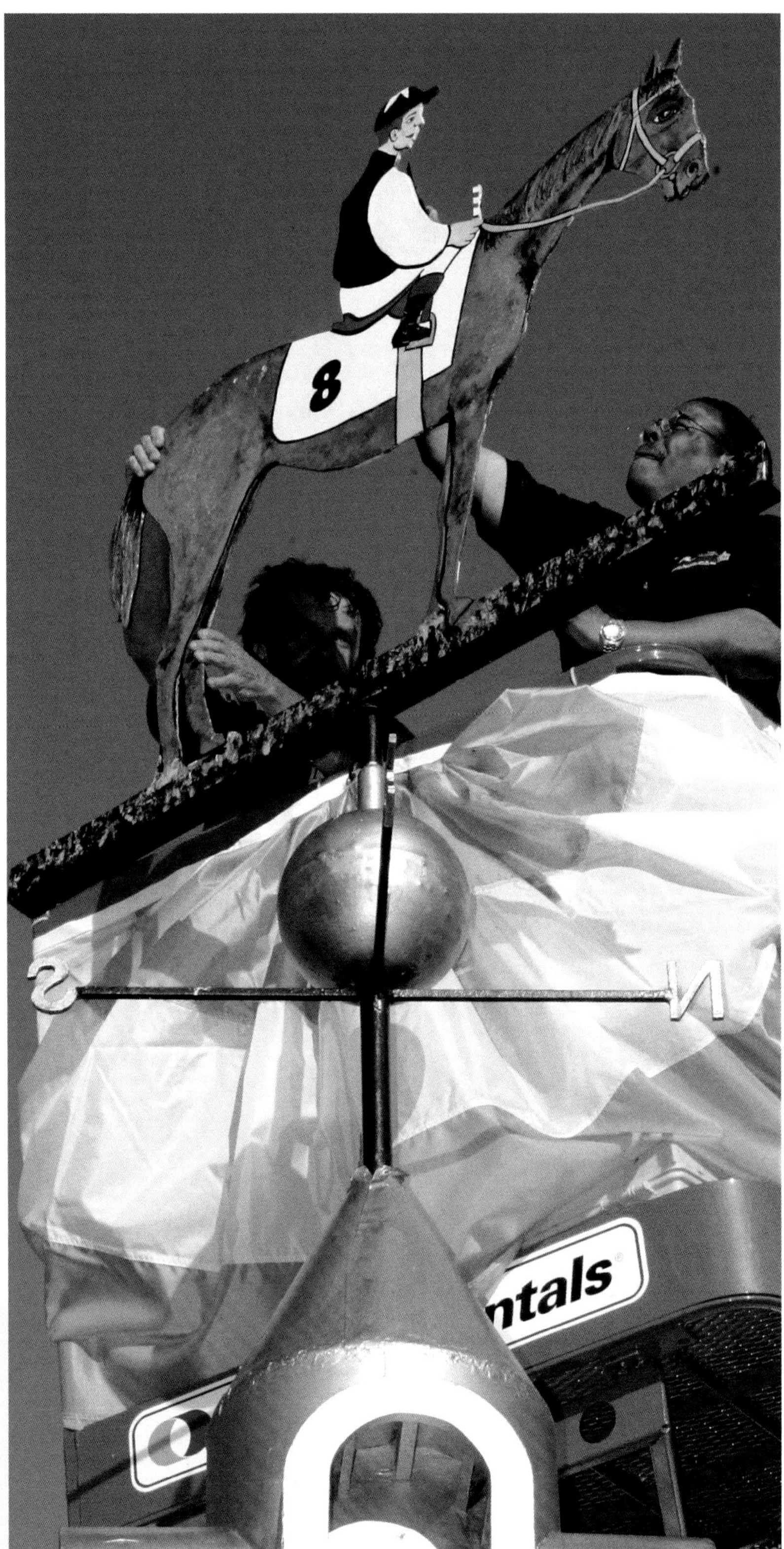

Right: *The horse weathervane in the winner's circle at Pimlico is shown being painted the new colours of the winning owner's silks. This is a tradition that is carried out immediately after the race has been won.*

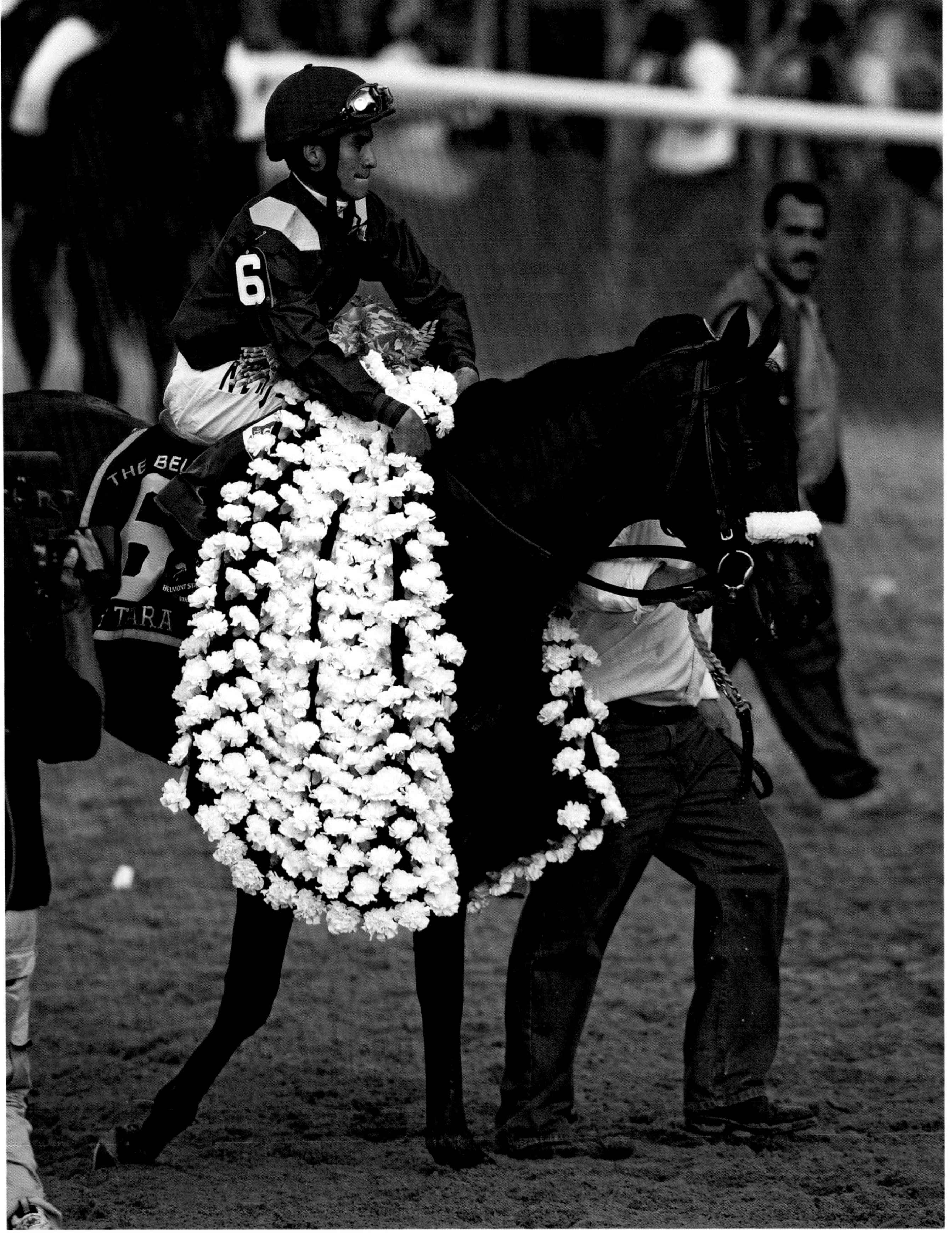

Left: *The third and final leg of the U.S. Triple Crown at Belmont Park, New York. Alan Garcia is victorious after winning aboard Da' Tara in 2008.*

Chapter 5: Mostest Hosses

It is sometimes said that a dog is a man's best friend, but the bond between humans and horses can also be strong. As British Prime Minister, Winston Churchill, once said, "The best thing for the inside of a man is the outside of a horse". Certainly there was a warm public response to the exploits of four outstanding thoroughbreds who raced between the First and Second World Wars.

This was a time of hardship for many, particularly in America after the 1929 Wall Street Crash heralded the Great Depression. There was a worldwide need for escapism and heroes – and Man o' War, Phar Lap, Hyperion and Seabiscuit all fitted the bill. These were racehorses who displayed abundant character as well as ability – and this was reflected by their legions of followers.

Man o' War and Phar Lap were chestnut giants who became nicknamed 'Big Red'. Man o' War, from his first race, was demonstrably a stars and stripes, all-American Hall of Famer, following in the hoof prints of Flying Childers, Eclipse and Lexington in lifting the thoroughbred species to another level. The antipodean Phar Lap matched his physique and possessed a heart of astonishing size, but took longer to find his raceday powers.

Left: *Seabiscuit became a symbol of hope to Americans in the years after the Great Depression. Here he is after winning the Pimlico Special in 1938 with trainer Tom Smith and owner C.S. Howard.*

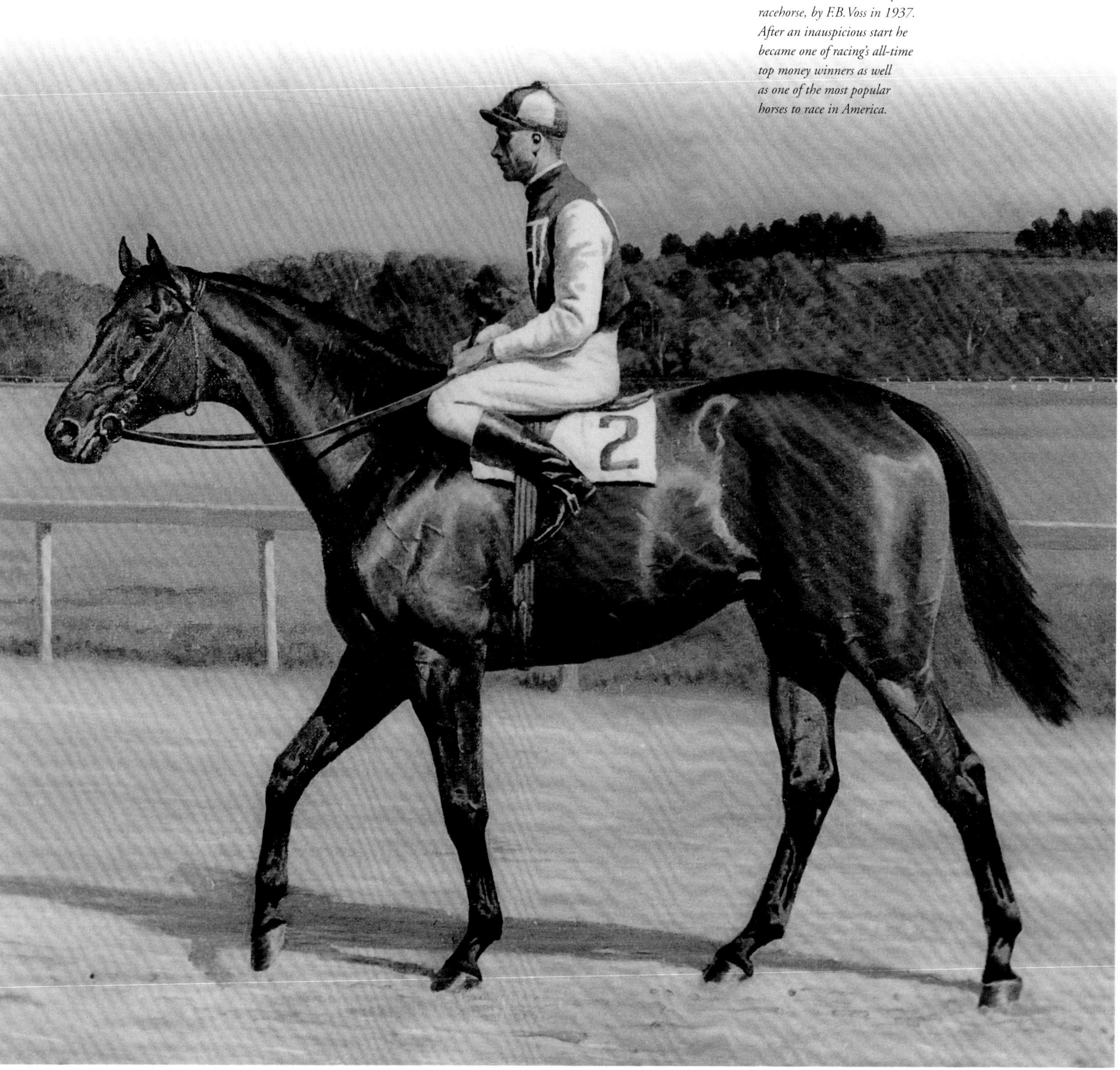

Below: *Seabiscuit – champion racehorse, by F.B. Voss in 1937. After an inauspicious start he became one of racing's all-time top money winners as well as one of the most popular horses to race in America.*

In comparison the laid back Hyperion and Seabiscuit were diminutive. However, that was part of their charm; that they slugged it out hoof to hoof with bigger colts and kept on winning. Certainly there is something alluring about high achievers, whether human or equine, who defy the odds, break records and are regularly first past the post.

Man o' War is still considered by many to be quite simply the greatest racehorse of all time. Sportswriter Grantland Rice wrote: "Man o' War was something different – something extra – as great a competitor as Ty Cobb, Jack Dempsey, Tommy Hitchcock, Ben Hogan or anyone else. He struck me always as one who had a furious desire to win – all the way with all he had."

Man o' War's doting groom, Will Harbut, summed it up even more succinctly, when he described him as the "mostest hoss that ever was," later explaining the decision to send him to stud by stating: "he broke all the records and he broke down all the horses so there wasn't nothing for him to do but retire".

He was bred and initially owned by August Belmont II, Chairman of the American Jockey Club. Belmont, at the age of sixty-five, felt compelled to serve in the United States Army in France during World War I. While he was overseas, his wife named a new foal 'Man o' War' in his honour. However, his unselfish and patriotic devotion to duty forced them to release their racing assets, an act that deserved a better side effect than selling off undiscovered equine gold on the cheap. Yet at the Saratoga yearling sale in 1918, Samuel D. Riddle purchased the bargain of all bargains and took Man o' War to his farm in Maryland.

Above: *Little Hyperion in Lord Derby's distinctive black and white colours in 1933. The horse's Epsom Derby win gave his owner a second victory in the event named after one of his ancestors.*

Left: *Big-hearted Phar Lap, pride of Australia; here at the AJC Derby at Randwick in 1929.*

The two-year-old made a winning debut at Belmont Park in 1919, and three weeks later added the Keene Memorial Stakes. But then came defeat in the Sanford Memorial Stakes, notable because it was to be his only one. When the starting tape was released Man o' War was still being circled with his back to the action and lost considerable ground on the field. Having got him turned round and racing, his jockey multiplied the initial error by riding him down cul-de-sacs where he became boxed in. Yet Man o' War still only lost by a rapidly diminishing half a length to the appropriately named Upset.

He finished his two-year-old campaign having won nine out of ten races. By the age of three he stood a strapping, muscular sixteen hands and two inches, weighed one thousand, one hundred and twenty-five pounds with a seventy-two inch girth and a fully extended stride of over nine yards.

He appeared primed to emulate Sir Barton who, one year before, had become the first winner of the U.S. Triple Crown. However, his protective owner, Samuel D. Riddle, thought the Kentucky Derby too early in the season for a young horse to race over a mile and a quarter. So this first leg was bypassed. This was unfortunate as the evidence of the other two legs suggested that he would have won the Triple Crown without breaking sweat.

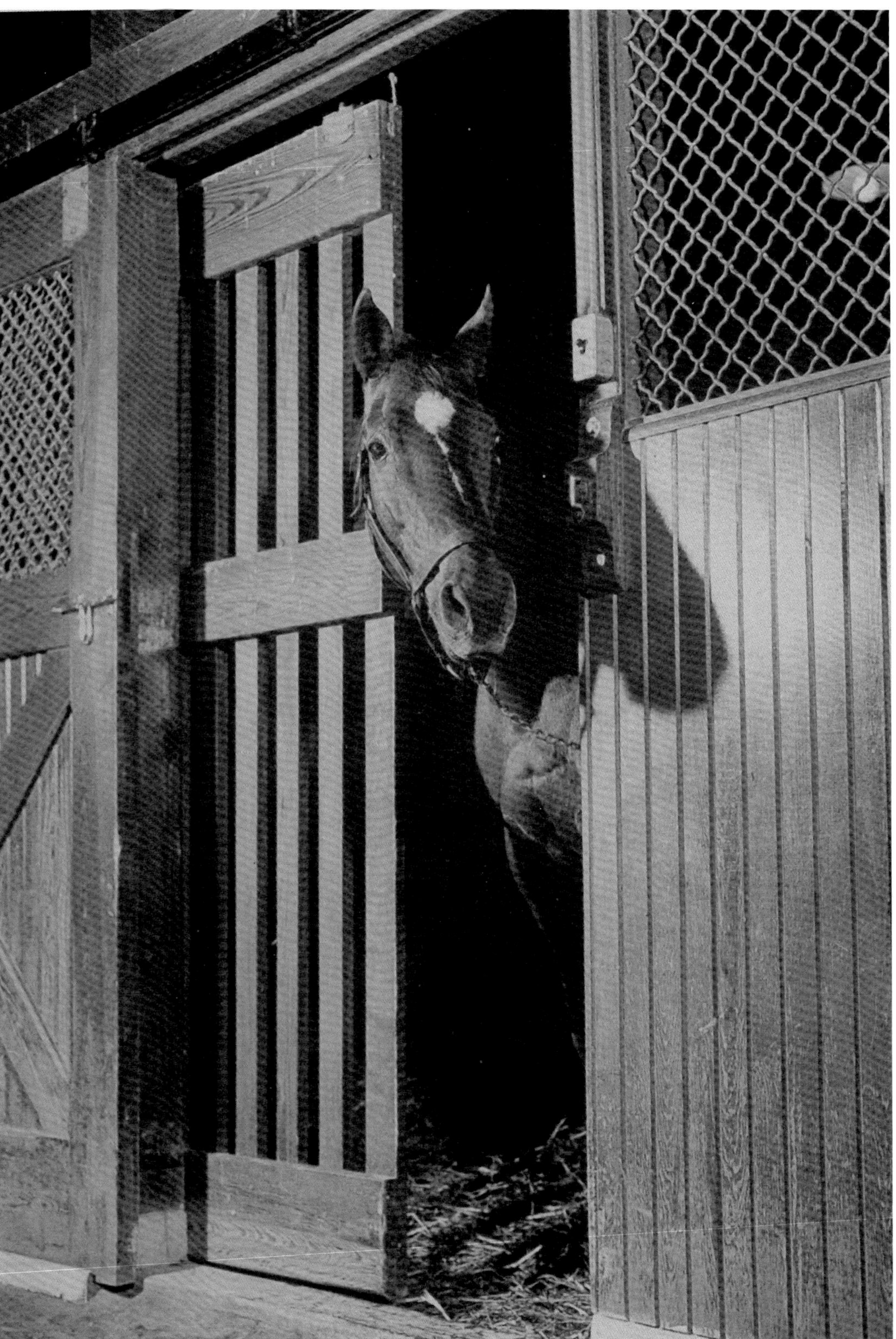

Right: *An all-American hero. Man o' War in his stable on his thirtieth birthday. The greatest racehorse ever?*

At the Preakness Stakes, in front of a record twenty-three thousand, he won with such ease that a sportswriter wrote: "It was not a race, only a performance. Those who saw it will not forget it." Then, at the Belmont Stakes, he cruised home twenty lengths ahead of his pursuers, setting an American time record. In both cases it was as though he was being unsaddled in the winning enclosure before the rest of the field had passed the winning post. These were not just victories but masterclasses.

That season he also won the Dwyer Stakes, the Travers Stakes, the Stuyvesant Handicap, the Jockey Club Gold Cup and the Lawrence Realization Stakes, the latter by a margin of one hundred lengths setting a world record for the distance. By now owners and trainers showed little appetite for the fight. In his final ten starts only fifteen horses in total lined up against him.

The end of Man o' War's glittering but brief racing career came in Canada's Kenilworth Park Gold Cup in a one and a quarter mile 'match race' against the Triple Crown winner, Sir Barton. Eagerly awaited, it proved to be a complete mismatch. Man o' War drew away in the first furlong, and won by seven lengths at a canter.

Below: *Phar Lap, 1931. Like Man o' War, Phar Lap was nicknamed 'Big Red'. Not only was his conformation large, but it housed a heart twice the normal size.*

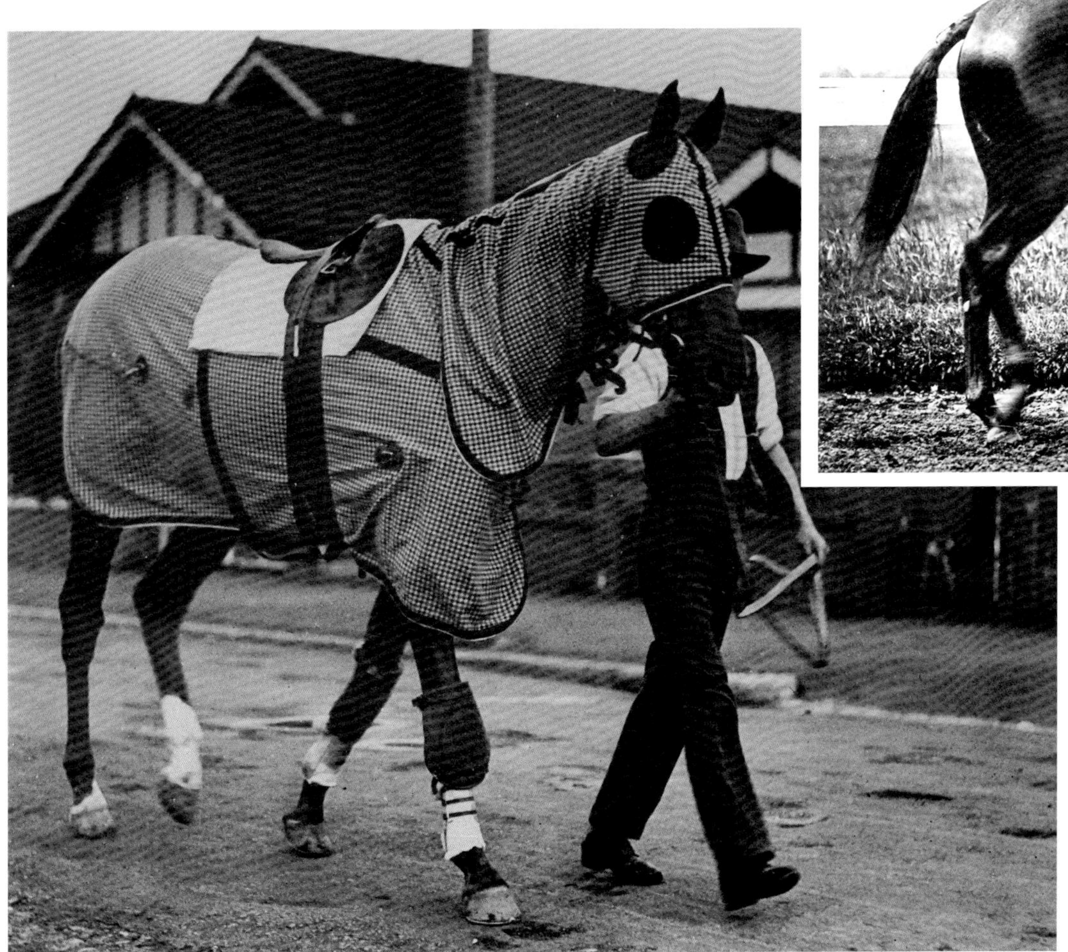

Left: *Man o' War gets to work at Belmont Park. His groom, Will Harbut, described him as "the mostest hoss that ever was".*

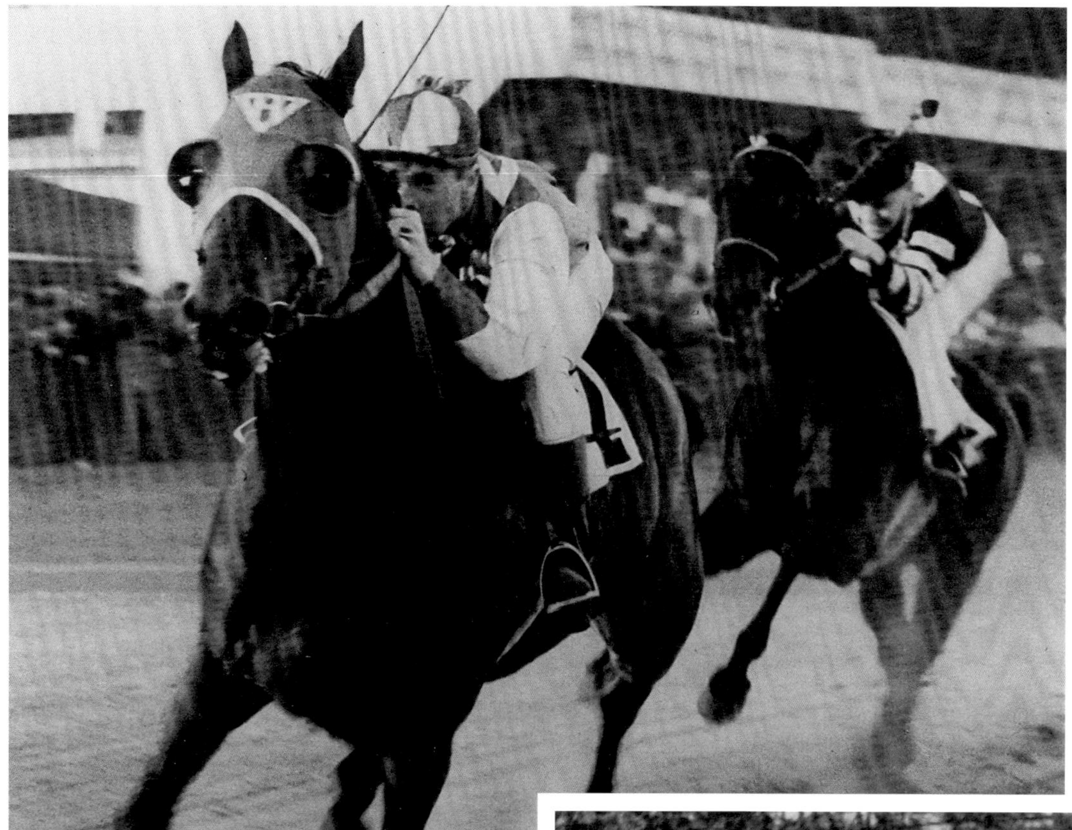

Left: *An epic race – Seabiscuit gets the better of his great rival, the U.S. Triple Crown winner, War Admiral, at Pimlico racecourse in 1938.*

Below: *A full-length profile of Seabiscuit in 1936. Nothing exceptional in his conformation, but what a winner he became.*

Following this undefeated season of eleven wins and a career that had amassed nearly a quarter of a million dollars in prize money, he stood at stud in Kentucky. Here, in twenty-two years, he produced more than sixty stakes winners and two hundred champions including War Admiral, who went on to win the U.S. Triple Crown in 1937.

When Man o' War died in 1947 – at the ripe old age of thirty – he was laid in state in his horsebox, in a coffin lined with the owner's black and gold racing colours. He now rests at the Kentucky Horse Park where his grave is marked with a life-sized bronze statue.

Like Man o' War, the Australian 'Big Red', Phar Lap, had heart. In fact when it was weighed after his death it was nearly twice as large as a normal horse's heart. Added to that physical advantage was his height. He stood a towering seventeen hands and one inch tall and possessed a girth which spanned seventy-nine inches. So height, heart and breadth aplenty. Whether he was blessed with good looks was a matter of debate because the young Phar Lap's chestnut face was covered with warts. His gait, too, was unathletic and faltering.

He never raced in his native New Zealand and moved to Australia after he was purchased at the Trentham Yearling Sales for one hundred and sixty guineas. Owner David J. Davis had been persuaded to buy the horse without a viewing by down-on-his-luck trainer, Harry Telford. But Davis was so underwhelmed when the horse first ambled in front of him that he refused to pay Telford to train him. The two compromised and agreed a deal that Telford would train for free but get two thirds of any winnings. Like Samuel D. Riddle and Man o' War, Telford had struck the deal of a lifetime.

What influenced Telford's thinking and gave him confidence was his knowledge of pedigree. He knew that Phar Lap had good genes, sired by Night Raid out of a dam called Entreaty, and had the extraordinary Melbourne Cup winner, Carbine, as one of his ancestors. So even if first impressions were not favourable, the pedigree was.

Telford also gelded Phar Lap, in the hope that the colt would focus on racing and earn prize money to offset against his training costs. At first it was all in vain. As a two-year-old he trailed in last in his first race and was unplaced in the next three. But gradually he began to warm to his task. He won the six-furlong Maiden Juvenile Handicap at Rosehill and was a fast finishing second in the Chelmsford Stakes at Randwick five months later.

And then, staggeringly, it all came together. Over the next two and half years he raced forty-one times and notched up thirty-six wins, three seconds and two thirds. Amazing consistency, amazing stamina, amazing performances – for most were high profile races against prominent opposition. He was now living up to the meaning of the name 'Phar Lap' which derived from the shared Zhan and Thai word for lightning.

As a three-year-old he won the AJC Plate and the Victoria Derby and finished third in the Melbourne Cup. The next year he won fourteen of sixteen races, which included the pinnacle of his career: the Melbourne Cup. Three days before he had won the Melbourne Stakes and someone (alleged to have been a bookmaker concerned at paying out vast amounts of money to winning gamblers) fired a shot at him as he was being returned to his stables. Hidden away for his own safety between meetings, the horse arrived at Flemington with an armed guard. Despite carrying a hefty nine stones, twelve pounds on his back, not to mention the expectation of thousands of punters who had backed him, he started as odds on favourite and cruised home by three lengths.

That massive frame of his won again two days after the Melbourne Cup and then again two days after that. Four races in eight days over five and three quarter miles – and all won. Phar Lap was a grafter who loved to run and had grown accustomed to winning.

As a five-year-old he won another seven races before a handicap of ten stone, ten pounds proved too much of a burden and he was unable to retain the Melbourne Cup in 1931. It was to be his last race in Australia and he was shipped to Mexico to compete in the Agua Caliente Handicap, targeting the largest purse ever raced for in North America. He won in a track-record time while carrying one hundred and twenty-nine pounds and became the third highest stake winner in the world.

Left: *Phar Lap in 1932. A horse with endless stamina and a fighting spirit that brought him many admirers.*

But in April 1932 his racing career and life came to an abrupt end, haemorrhaging to death with an inflamed stomach and intestines. Conspiracy theories suggested that he might have been deliberately poisoned, possibly by arsenic, possibly by U.S. gangsters who feared he would inflict further losses on their illegal bookmakers. Conjecture aside, Australia grieved the premature loss of a national treasure.

Jockey, Jim Pike, described Phar Lap as "the best I've ridden. In fact I don't think there has ever been his equal, certainly not during my time and before that either. I would say that up to a mile and a half Phar Lap is the best horse that Australia and one of the best the world's ever had. It's sacrilege, really, to ride some horses after once having been on Phar Lap's back."

His mounted hide, prepared by a New York taxidermist, is displayed at the Melbourne Museum, his skeleton at the Museum of New Zealand Te Papa Tongarewa and his fourteen and a half pound heart at the National Museum of Australia in Canberra.

In the same year as Phar Lap's Melbourne Cup triumph, on the other side of the planet, a tiny foal was born in the stables of the seventeenth Earl of Derby in Newmarket, England.

A chestnut with four white feet (a bad omen according to racing folklore) he was too diminutive and frail to eat his grain with the others, so a feed bunker was custom made. How would he ever be robust enough to make a racehorse? Thought was given to having him put down but trainer George Lambton was "impressed with his beautiful action and by his head, so full of character and courage". Thus the weakling was spared.

Called Hyperion after a Greek sun god, he barely topped fifteen hands when he went into training and matured at just fifteen hands, one and a half inches. And not only was he small, but he was lazy. He had to be worked hard to get fit but on the racecourse it became apparent that he was a star in the making.

Left: *Hyperion, 1933. A much smaller conformation, almost a pony, but what he lacked in size he made up for in sheer speed across the turf.*

In his second start as a two-year-old, he won the New Stakes over five furlongs at Ascot, breaking the course record. The next three races brought a dead heat, third and an easy victory in Newmarket's Dewhurst Stakes, traditionally a race that highlights those that will excel as three-year-olds.

Yet, over the winter Hyperion grew little and was disappointing in his dawn 'work'. So the Two Thousand Guineas was bypassed and he started in May with a two-length victory in the Chester Vase; though even then it required a sharp crack of the jockey's whip to shock him out of his winter doziness.

This made Hyperion a starting favourite for Epsom's blue riband event. So his victory was not entirely unexpected. However, to see the horse, carrying Lord Derby's famous black jacket and white cap, cruise home by four lengths in a record-breaking time took the breath away. It gave Lord Derby his second win in the event named by his ancestors, and made little Hyperion a public hero.

In the Prince of Wales' Stakes at Royal Ascot he won again, and then in the final English classic – the St Leger – he led from the start and romped home. He had been unbeaten as a three-year-old, securing two classics in the process.

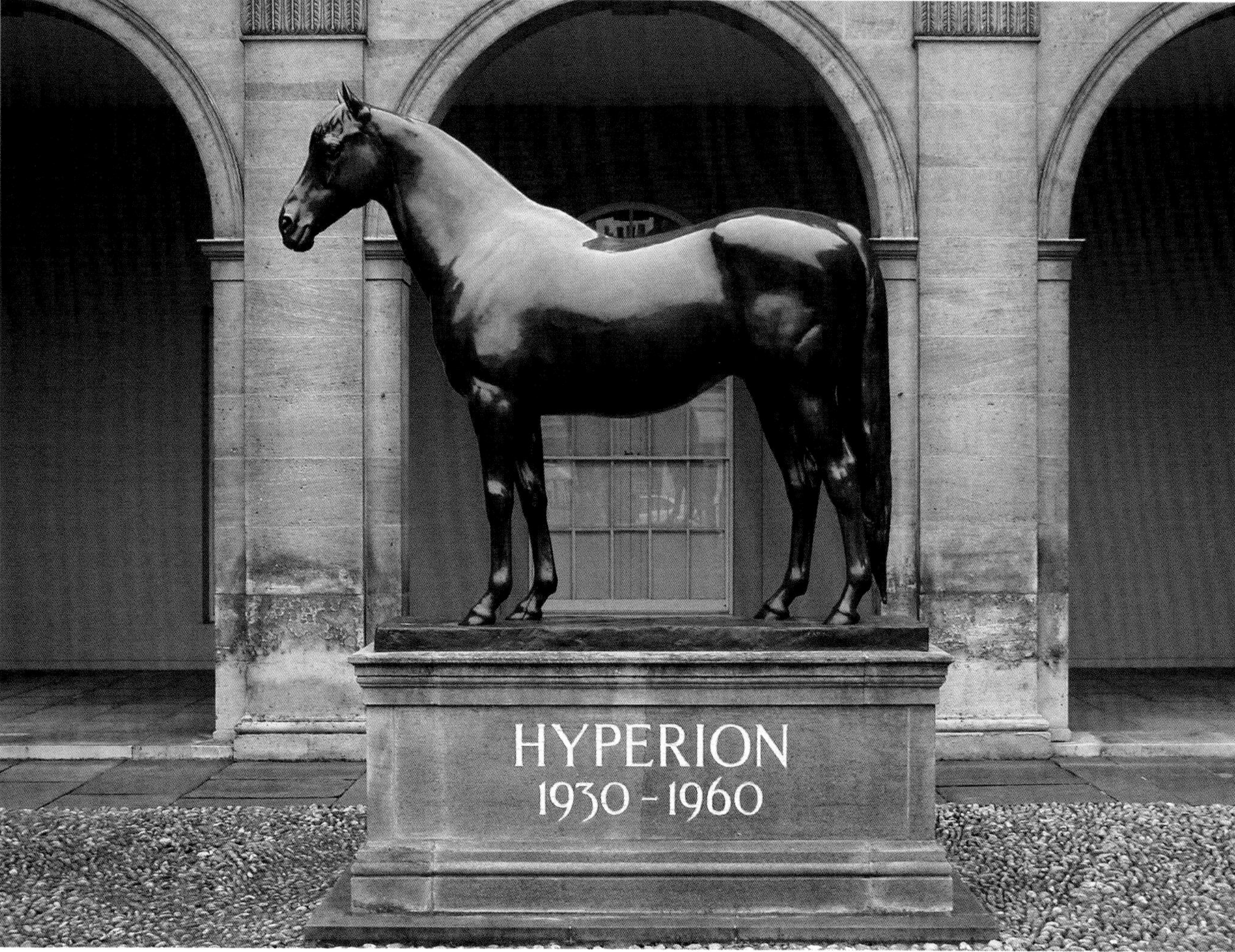

Left: *The magnificent statue of Hyperion that stands outside the offices of the Jockey Club in Newmarket, England. Many of the outstanding horses have statues in their honour.*

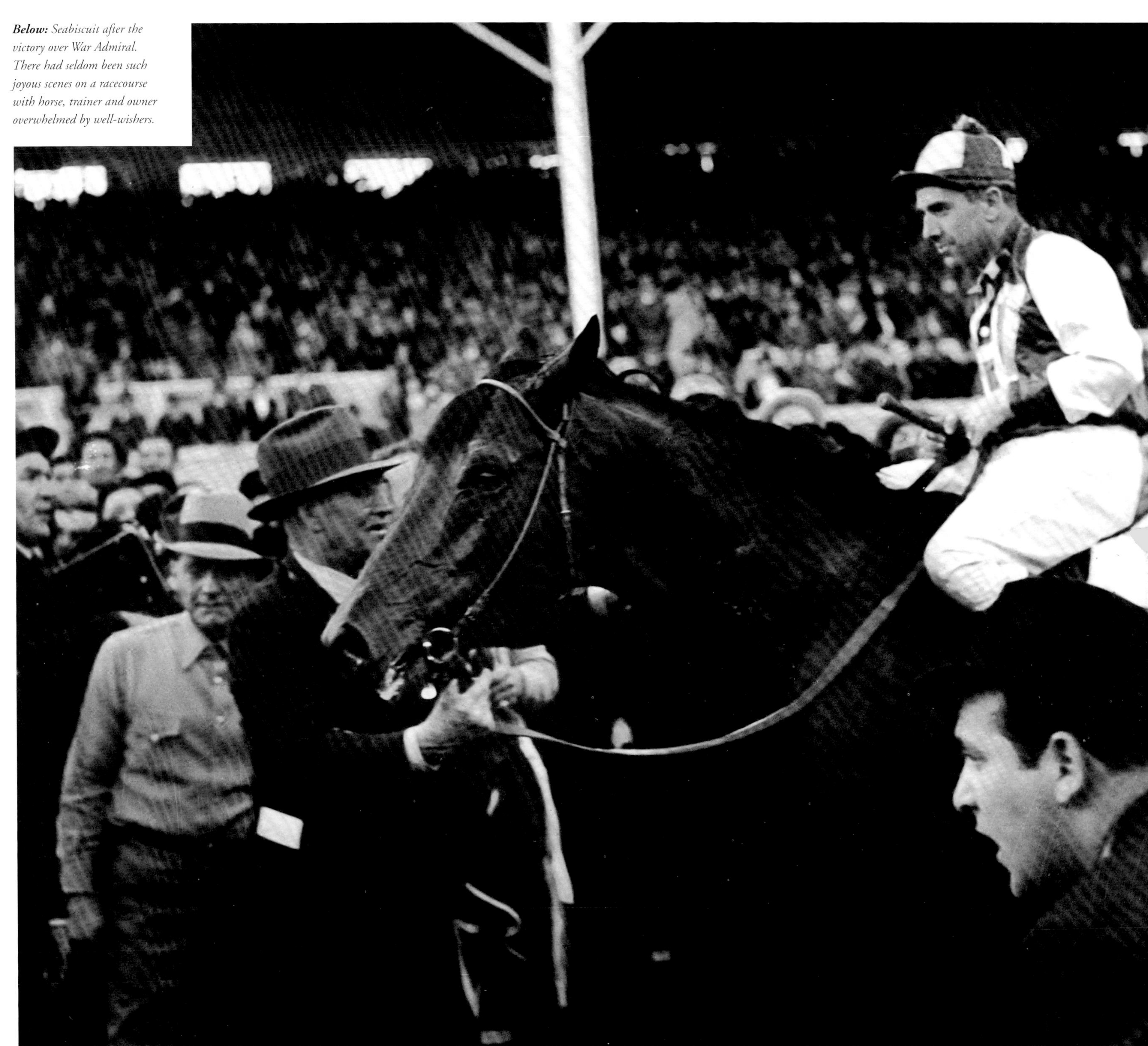

Below: *Seabiscuit after the victory over War Admiral. There had seldom been such joyous scenes on a racecourse with horse, trainer and owner overwhelmed by well-wishers.*

Next year, following a change of trainer, he was less outstanding and retired to Lord Derby's Woodland Stud in 1935 with a final record of nine wins in thirteen starts.

He spent most of his remaining life here (fascinated, it is said, by aeroplanes, which he would follow across the sky) siring five hundred and twenty-seven foals, of which one hundred and eighteen won stakes including seven winners of eleven English classics, as well as the Kentucky Derby and Preakness Stakes winner, Pensive, in the United States of America. Hyperion's statue stands outside the Jockey Club Rooms in his hometown of Newmarket.

It was uncanny how the baton of great racehorses was passed on. In the same year as Hyperion's Derby victory, a horse called Seabiscuit was born in the United States.

His paternal grandsire was Man o' War but when Seabiscuit was foaled in 1933 early indications of his physique were not encouraging. He was certainly no Man o' War; indeed he shared Hyperion's traits of being small, slender and sluggish. He liked to sleep and he liked to eat; moreover he was knobbly-kneed and unattractive to the eye. These negative character traits encouraged his trainer, 'Sunny Jim' Fitzsimmons, to use him mainly as a workmate for the star of the stable, Omaha. There was nothing unusual about Seabiscuit. He seemed a commonplace horse and at first ran in low profile races, the first ten of which he never looked like winning.

Left: *Hyperion winds down after his Derby win at Jack Killalee's stables at Epsom. Hyperion could be lazy in the yard, but on racedays he came alive and possessed an exhilarating turn of speed.*

As a three-year-old he was given a gruelling workload, racing no less than thirty-five times, and on his eighteenth attempt he was finally first past the post. He won four more times that year but was less than inspiring through the next season, and his owners jettisoned him to automobile entrepreneur Charles S. Howard for just eight thousand dollars.

This was the turning point for Seabiscuit. His new trainer, Tom Smith, seemed to connect with the horse's unusual psyche, and unorthodox training methods made a difference. His new jockey, Canadian Johnny 'Red' Pollard, also seemed able, in racing parlance, to 'get a tune' out of him. Consequently, in nine races in America's East, Seabiscuit won frequently – and his last two races of the year, just south of San Francisco, hinted at a bright future. He won the Bay Bridge Handicap – carrying a top weight of one hundred and sixteen pounds – by five lengths, and then won the World's Fair Handicap.

In 1937, he finished a close run second in February's Santa Anita Handicap, California's most prestigious race, and his improvement thereafter was marked. He won five times at various venues around America between 26th June and 7th August; each one a stakes race, despite carrying heavier weight handicaps. Through 1937 Seabiscuit won eleven of his fifteen races and became the country's leading money winner.

On the West Coast in particular, his rags to riches story made him an unlikely champion and a symbol of hope to many in the desperate grip of the Great Depression and the threat of another World War. His races were followed on radio and newsreel and filled hundreds of column inches in the newspapers. Howard, with his business acumen, fanned the flames, marketing merchandise to the fans.

In 1938, as a five-year-old, Seabiscuit's success continued, though his jockey, Pollard, had to be replaced after injury. George Woolf, a great rider and old friend of Pollard, took over the reins.

The media and public wanted an old-fashioned 'match race' with the U.S. Triple Crown winner War Admiral, also sired by Man o' War – and, on 1st November 1938, they got their wish. Seabiscuit represented America's West, War Admiral the East and they raced over one and three sixteenth miles at the Pimlico racecourse. Despite being staged on a Tuesday, trains were scheduled from all over the country to transport followers to the racetrack. Forty thousand attended, with another forty million tuning in to the radio.

Seabiscuit created a length advantage in the early stages. But down the back straight the Triple Crown champion – and favourite for the race – cut into the lead, drew level and momentarily moved ahead before Seabiscuit pulled away again and continued to extend his lead over the closing stretch, finally winning by four lengths. It was an astonishing and much acclaimed victory that embroidered the Seabiscuit legend.

Serious injury kept Seabiscuit away from the racetrack through most of 1939, but he returned in 1940 and ended his career – now back under jockey 'Red' Pollard who had also courageously recovered from his injuries – with victory in the Santa Anita Handicap in front of seventy-eight thousand racegoers. Bedlam followed his win. Seabiscuit had become racing's all-time leading money winner as well as one of the most popular horses to race in America.

His stud career was moderate, but over five thousand visitors made the pilgrimage to Ridgewood Ranch to see him in the seven years before his death. His burial site is a secret to this day, known only to his owner's family.

Right: *Canadian jockey 'Red' Pollard holds a microphone up to the mouth of winning racehorse Seabiscuit, 1938. The two were good for each other with Pollard able to 'get a tune' out of the remarkable horse better than most.*

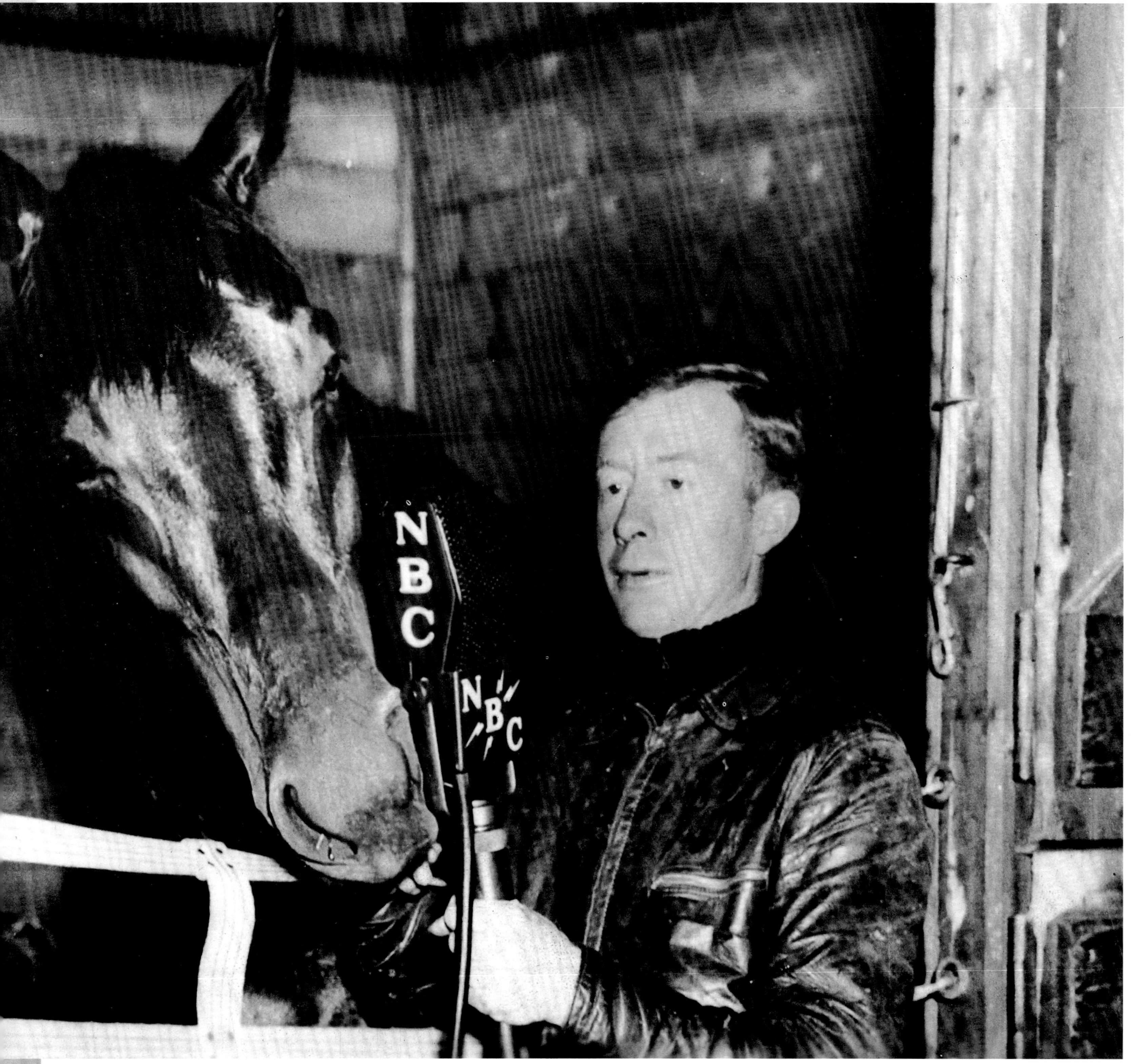
NBC
NBC

Chapter 6: Soft Hands, Cotton Fingers

Down the centuries a minimum requirement for each and every jockey has been the strength of mind and discipline to cope with three hardships that accompany race riding every bit as much as do stirrups and a saddle.

The first of these hardships is the travelling. The nature of this has changed down the years – it is safe to assume that Francis Buckle's modes of transport in the eighteenth century were significantly different to those of a modern-day globe-trotter like Frankie Dettori. Nevertheless, the racecourses have never come to the rider, so they have always had to be constantly on the move.

The second hardship is the ever-present danger. Every time they get on board, risk rides with them and an ambulance travels in their wake like a vulture sensing blood. When jockeys fall it is usually at a speed of around thirty-five miles an hour, so the impact can be bone-breaking and, sometimes, career-ending. One of the sport's finest, Australian Damien Oliver, lost both his father and brother to premature deaths whilst race-riding.

Below: *A tight finish looks likely on the all-weather surface at Wolverhampton racecourse in England. An opportunity for the top jockeys to give their mount an edge in the run in, where races are won and lost by fractions of a second.*

Finally, they have to maintain both an unnaturally low weight and an athlete's condition and vigour on the most minimal diet. Their career hangs in the balance every time they register on the weighing room scales as owners and trainers soon discard jockeys who carry excess pounds. So, put simply, most have to starve.

In addition, the top jockeys require a range of attributes, one of which can lead to unpopularity. The likes of Fred Archer and Lester Piggott could be utterly ruthless in obtaining the ride they wanted and Piggott once summed up the need: "It is part of a jockey's job to get on to the best horses, and if that involves ruffling a few feathers, so be it."

Right: *The dreaded scales. Trainers and owners always want weight to be taken off their horses, so the lighter the jockey the better. Most are continually on a diet.*

Below: *Steve Donoghue drives Humorist to the front in the 1921 Epsom Derby. Donoghue at Epsom was always a formidable foe. He had a full understanding of the unique, rollercoaster terrain and employed his experience and race-riding skills to advantage.*

Once on board, their craft can be showcased. When a one thousand and five hundred pound thoroughbred covers the ground at speed, the only parts of the jockey's anatomy in contact are the inside of his feet and his ankles. Coordination, reflexes, balance and strength are minimum requirements, along with horse sense – that instinctive ability to think like the animal, sensing their mood and courage, cajoling them into giving their best. This is difficult to identify in others and impossible to coach. Some jockeys just have it; an uncanny ability to establish a rapport and put the thoroughbred at ease. They seem to do little, indeed they scarcely move. Yet when horse and rider move away they are in harmony, a union rather than two individual identities.

This skill was well described when it was written of Steve Donoghue: "There is a physical as well as a spiritual side to Steve's success. It is called balance. Watch him coming down the hill at Epsom. You never see him holding on to the reins as many of his colleagues are compelled to. His touch is as light downhill as it is on the flat, and that I believe is why he is so successful on the Downs course. His mounts have never any shifting dead weight to carry."

Last but not least, jockeys need to think well, with a brain that is cool, clear and bright, even in the thick of the action.

Below: *Frank Buckle (on the left in the cap) along with owner breeder John Wastell, trainer Robert Robson and a lad. Buckle was nicknamed a 'pocket Hercules' and won 27 classics.*

Above: *A painting by B. Marshall that depicts some of the prominent jockeys in the nineteenth century – Sam Chifney, Wheatley and Jem Robinson. Robinson won Newmarket's Two Thousand Guineas a record nine times.*

One of the first to display this cocktail of characteristics was England's 'pocket Hercules', Francis Buckle, born the son of a Newmarket saddler in 1766. He rode his first race at the age of twelve – weighing three stone, thirteen pounds – and went on to win twenty-seven classics. He rode till he was sixty-five and died the following year. Jem Robinson won the Two Thousand Guineas nine times, which remains a record; Elnathan Flatman was champion jockey between 1840 and 1852 and George Fordham took over the mantle between 1855 and 1863 and then five more times after that. In all he won sixteen classics. Of Fordham, it was said that he "rode with fairly short leathers, got well down on his mount's back, and slewed his head and body almost sideways during a race with his shoulders hunched up high".

So there had been renowned jockeys for a while but it was in the last quarter of the nineteenth century that they began to lodge themselves in the sport's consciousness. For that we can thank the great, tragic Fred Archer who achieved so much, so young, in England with thirteen consecutive titles and then put a shotgun to his head in the mists of mental and physical misery.

A contemporary across the Atlantic also achieved much and died young. Indeed, Isaac Murphy was to be dubbed 'the coloured Archer'. Born in 1861 in Kentucky, Murphy won his local Derby three times amongst six hundred and twenty-eight overall wins at a remarkable success rate of forty-four per cent. Sadly he died of pneumonia in 1896 at the age of thirty-five. He is buried next to Man o' War at the Kentucky Horse Park's entrance.

Above: *Isaac Murphy, dubbed the 'coloured Archer'. The Kentucky-born Murphy was perhaps the first great American jockey and won 44 per cent of the races in which he rode. Alas, like Archer, he died young.*

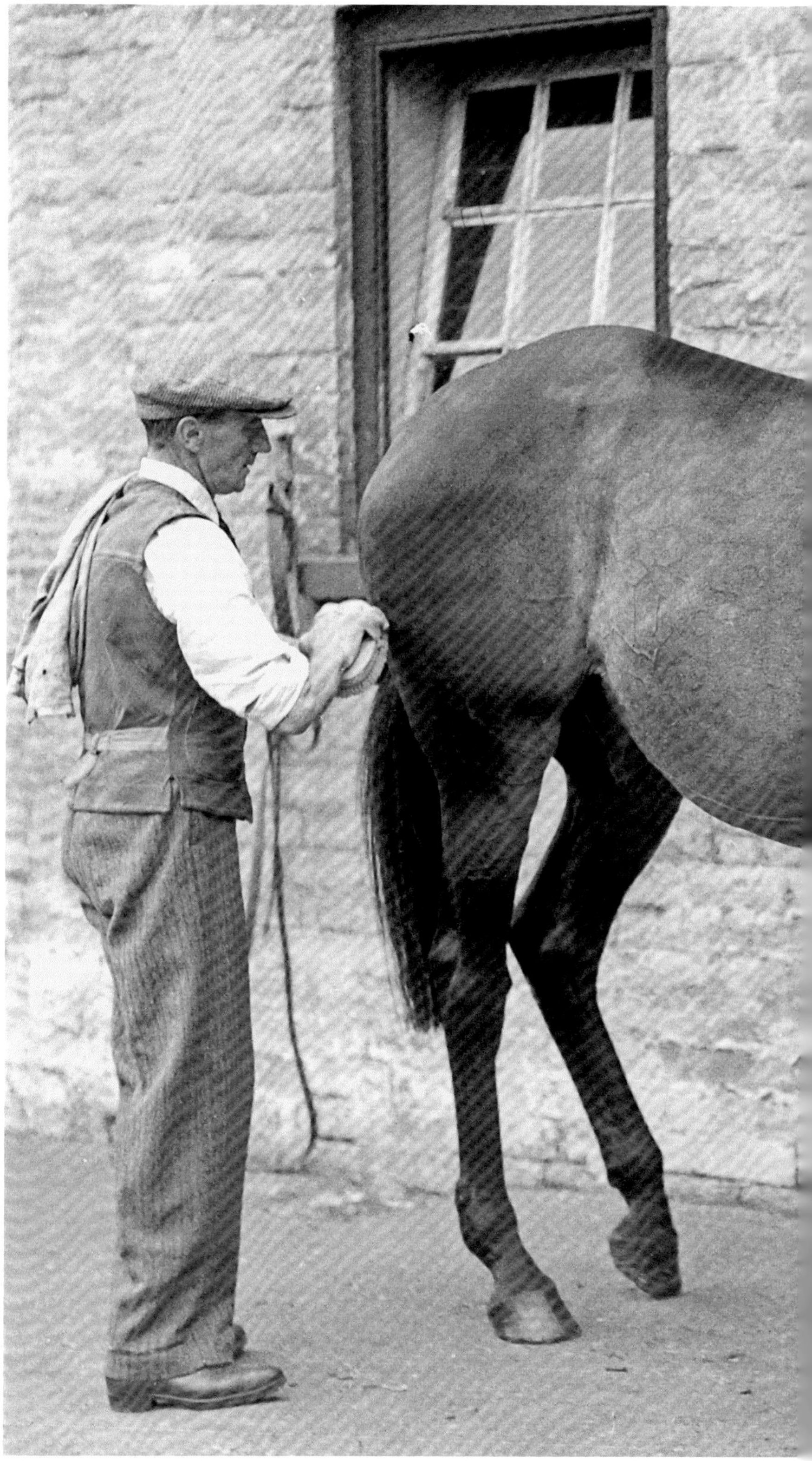

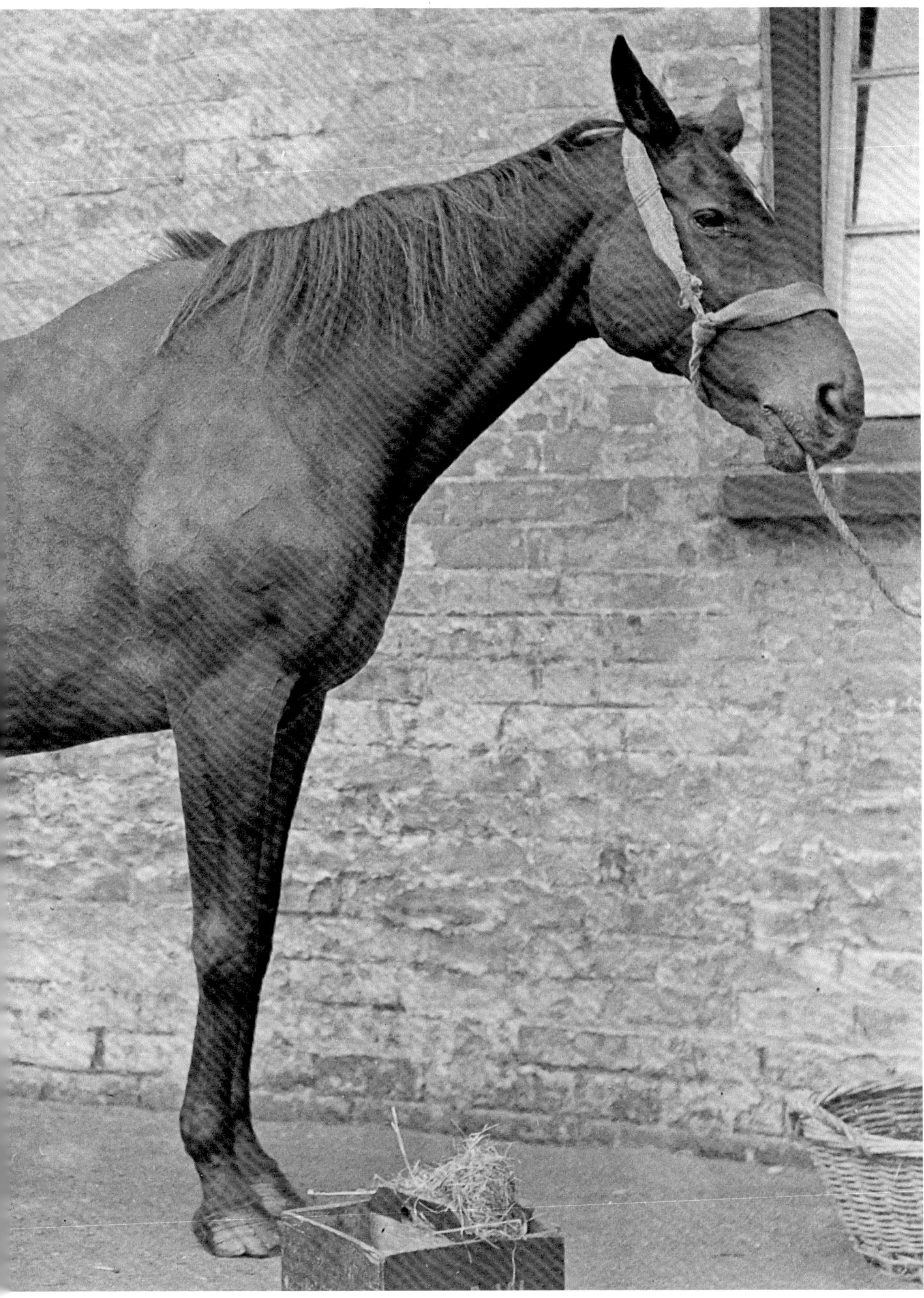

Archer and Murphy's time in the sun, alas, was all too brief but they started the trend that certain jockeys would dominate the record books for a while, their star shining bright, before handing over the reins to the next era.

For instance, Archer's mantle in Britain was taken on by Steve Donoghue in the period up to and after the First World War. He was champion jockey ten consecutive times between 1914 and 1923 and rode the acclaimed Brown Jack to six consecutive wins in the Queen Alexandra Stakes at Royal Ascot. However, he was most at home on Epsom's Downs on Derby Day.

Left: *The acclaimed Brown Jack achieved six consecutive wins at Royal Ascot having started life as a hurdler. You can sense his power in this photograph. In addition, he was fortunate to have Steve Donoghue on his back so regularly.*

HISTORY IN THE MAKING
America, 1959–1966

Horse racing on the flat is a sport in a hurry. The turbo-charged races are over in a couple of minutes, and particularly in the modern era thoroughbred careers do not seem to last much longer. Two-year-old hopefuls may be put out to stud not much more than a season later. Some leave memories, yet they are fireworks that fizz and sparkle briefly then are gone.

But there should always be space to appreciate the old-fashioned qualities of durability, longevity and consistency – and on that score few can match the record of Kentucky's Kelso. He raced sixty-three times in eight years, 1959 to 1966 inclusive, and won thirty-nine times, including many top-class races.

Although none of these were Triple Crown contests he was voted fourth in the top one hundred thoroughbred champions of the twentieth century by Blood-Horse magazine (behind Man o' War, Secretariat and Citation). He was also Male Horse of the Year in America in 1960 (for three-year-olds), 1961, 1962, 1963 and 1964, the only five-time winner in history.

Foaled in 1957, Kelso was a handful and was gelded to calm him down. He never lost his spark, though, and made his debut in 1959 as a two-year-old, winning his first race, followed by two seconds. These were low-profile races but there were traces of promise.

A new trainer, Carl Hanford, meant that the U.S. Triple Crown was done and dusted by the time Kelso took to the track as a three-year-old. He won on his first outing for Hanford, who liked what he saw: "He was an extremely determined horse. If he saw a horse in front, he wanted to get to him. You could take him back or send him to the front. He was an extremely sound horse who was light on his feet with incredible balance. Kelso could wheel on a dime, spinning round in a circle and never letting his feet touch each other."

Above: *'King Kelly' Kelso wins again. He competed on fourteen racetracks and won in six states so that by his retirement as a nine-year-old he had become racing's all-time leading money winner.*

That season he won nine out of ten starts, including the first of five consecutive victories in the Jockey Club Gold Cup, the most in a major stakes race of any horse in history.

As a four-year-old he won the New York Handicap Triple, made up of the Metropolitan Handicap, Suburban Handicap and the Brooklyn Handicap. And so he went on, season after season, accompanied by a loyal entourage of groom Lawrence Fitzpatrick, work rider Dick Jenkins, and a dog called Charlie Potatoes.

His performances at the age of five and six were exemplary and his popularity snowballed with every outing, the public able to get to know and love him because of his longevity. He had his own fan club and his own nickname: 'King Kelly'. In all Kelso competed on fourteen tracks and won in six states. When Hanford retired him at the age of nine, Kelso was racing's all-time leading money winner. In sixty-three starts he was out of the money only ten times.

As a gelding, Kelso could not be retired to stud. Instead, he went on to a second career as a hunter and a show jumper. He died in 1983 at the age of twenty-six, a horse with true staying power.

***Right:** Kelso's longevity and achievements brought him admirers from all around the globe. Here, at the Laurel racecourse he provides an audience to a trainer and jockey, from Russia.*

One newspaper article of the time stated, "The reason why Donoghue always distinguishes himself at Epsom is that he is so clever at getting off and gets going so well that he is rarely if ever bunched in going downhill… Donoghue knows every inch of the track at Epsom and his presence on a horse is the equivalent of lightening the animal's weight by at least seven pounds."

He won the Derby six times including consecutive wins on Humorist (1921), Captain Cuttle (1922) and Papyrus (1923) and perhaps Donoghue would be regarded as Britain's best-ever jockey if it were not for two legends who followed.

The first 'legend' rode ponies bareback almost as soon as he could walk, and by the age of seven he drove the pony and trap passenger service run by his family. He became a stable boy at fifteen and his riding skills and style – using a long rein and an upright stance – soon became commented on, leading to apprentice rides. The boy, Gordon Richards, became a fully-fledged professional jockey in 1925 – just after Donoghue's dominance had begun to wane – and immediately became a champion.

But no sooner had the twenty-one-year-old's career taken off than he contracted the debilitating disease, tuberculosis. He was sent to the English countryside to recover in a sanatorium – as was the custom in those days – and progress was slow. However, the boy became soul mates with a patient, Bill Rowell, who recognized that he was destined for wealth and fame and provided invaluable guidance and support.

Left: *Field streaming in his wake at last, Sir Gordon Richards eases Pinza to the 1953 Epsom Derby, having suffered twenty-seven previous failures. This was Richards's swan song and ensured he retired with a full and unblemished record to his name.*

Rowell's assessment proved to be spot on. Once Richards had fully recovered there was no stopping him or the horses that he rode. In 1932 he became stable jockey to trainer Fred Darling and broke the longstanding record for the number of wins in one season with two hundred and fifty-nine wins in 1933.

What followed was the race-by-race creation of a mountain of statistics: champion jockey no less than twenty-six times; four thousand, eight hundred and seventy winners. However, as retirement loomed there was one notable gap on his record. He had never won the Epsom Derby, despite twenty-seven attempts.

His opportunity to put the record straight came in 1953, the year of Queen Elizabeth II's Coronation when he rode the giant Pinza. Four days earlier he had become the first (and, so far, the only) jockey to be knighted in recognition of his 'services to racing'. Having taken the lead with two furlongs to go he was swept to the finishing post on a tidal wave of acclaim. The long-awaited win was celebrated by the sporting nation, not least the new Queen who summoned him from the winning enclosure to pass on her congratulations.

And so when a pelvis injury accelerated his move into training at the age of fifty-one, he left with an unblemished, comprehensive list of achievements. No regrets to haunt him. No ifs, buts or maybes.

Yet if the 1953 Derby was Richards's swan song and hearty farewell to an adoring public, then 1954 saw the passing of the baton and the fanfared announcement of a new household name as the precocious eighteen-year-old, Lester Piggott, won on Never Say Die.

Right: *The year after Sir Gordon Richards rode Pinza to the Epsom Derby, the young Lester Piggott announced his prodigious talent to the sporting world on board Sir Ivor, seen following victory.*

***Above:** A contented, winning smile from the ace jockey from Wagga Wagga, Australia, Scobie Breasley. Breasley was a stylist able to adapt to different conditions around the globe.*

Piggott had racing in the genes. His father, Keith, was a jockey and trainer, and his grandfather rode the winners of two Grand Nationals. The young Lester won his first race at the age of twelve, standing just four feet, six inches and weighing five stone, four pounds. He grew, though, to five feet, eight inches – tall for a flat racing jockey – and so had to endure a spartan dietary regime to keep his weight down to around eight stone. Nevertheless he rode to nine Derby victories, thirty wins in the English classics and was champion jockey eleven times. Overall his first and last victories spanned forty-five years.

Even now images of 'The Long Fellow' in the saddle remain easily in the mind of those who saw him: the familiar tight-cheeked, waxwork face; a tall figure riding incredibly short with his backside stuck high in the air, a style that was subsequently widely adopted. Sportswriter Hugh McIlvanney wrote: "With his face lined like a map of hard roads travelled, his capacity for pulverizing put downs and the inspired audacity of his jockeyship, he became one of the most magical presences in sport over the last fifty years."

In fact it was an Australian who provided one of the strongest challenges to Piggott's supremacy, one Arthur Edward Breasley – more commonly known as 'Scobie' after the famous Australian trainer James Scobie – from Wagga Wagga in New South Wales.

Coincidentally, Breasley had been married on the same day, 5th November 1935, that Piggott was born. Breasley was one of the first globe-trotting jockeys. He rode three thousand two hundred and fifty-one winners in his native Australia and another two thousand, one hundred and sixty-one winners in England, where he was champion jockey four times.

Amongst these wins were international nuggets: Australia's Caulfield Cup, England's Epsom Derby twice (both after he had passed the age of fifty) and France's Prix de l'Arc de Triomphe.

It was Breasley's technique that allowed him to adapt to differing conditions. He was impeccably balanced in the saddle and used hands and heels to ease his mount forward, seldom resorting to the whip. As Ron Hutchinson, another Australian jockey, opined, "He had a beautiful seat in the saddle and a lovely style. As well as that he was totally fearless and I remember that sometimes, when I was following him, he would take an opening that weren't there and get up to win by a head."

George Moore was another Australian with a light touch – he was nicknamed 'Cotton-fingers' – who tried his luck in England. Trainer Neville Begg said, "George Moore was a great horseman, who had a touch of genius about him. He rode a lot of winners for me and I was amazed at the way he always placed his horses so well during races."

Right: *George Moore unsaddles Fleet after winning the One Thousand Guineas at Newmarket. Like Breasley, Moore employed his talent over several countries. Both possessed those ideal traits in a horseman: "soft hands and cotton fingers".*

Like Breasley, Moore's success spanned across France, Australia and England. Big wins included the Prix de l'Arc de Triomphe in 1959 and a purple spell when, in 1967, he added the One Thousand Guineas on Fleet, and the Two Thousand Guineas and Epsom Derby on Royal Palace. On home soil he was champion jockey in Sydney on ten occasions between 1957 and 1969, won the AJC Derby six times and rode Tulloch, one of Australia's finest racehorses, in a career boasting two thousand, two hundred and seventy-eight victories.

If the Australians, Breasley and Moore, were known for their craftsmanship then the American Eddie Arcaro, the son of an impoverished taxi driver in Ohio, was more overtly forceful. This was typified by his trademark stick up, head down, arms pumping, full on charges to the line. Indeed in the rawness of his youth he could be hot-tempered and reckless, and was banned for a year after deliberately colliding with rival Vincent Nordarse during a race. Afterwards, the unrepentant Arcaro claimed that he was trying to kill Nordarse. However, with age he mellowed without ever losing that all-consuming desire to be first past the post. He won more American 'classics' than any other jockey and is the only one to have won the U.S. Triple Crown twice, with Whirlaway in 1941 and Citation in 1948. He also has five Kentucky Derbys to his name and six wins in both of the subsequent legs of the Triple Crown.

Above: *All-American heroes with plenty to laugh about. Willie Shoemaker and Eddie Arcaro share a joke together. Their riding styles were vastly different but were hugely effective.*

"There were great jockeys before he came onto the scene," wrote Joe Hirsch in the *Daily Racing Form*. "There are great ones riding today. There will be great ones in the future. But whenever men gather to speak of racing and race riding, Eddie Arcaro always will be 'the master'."

Americans who beg to differ probably side with the diminutive – even by jockeys' standards – Bill Shoemaker. Excessive weight was never an issue for Shoemaker. When he was born in Texas in 1931 he weighed just two and a half pounds. Medics were pessimistic. They did not expect the newborn to last the night, but placed him in a shoebox in a lightly heated oven to keep him warm. Of course he survived and went on to become four feet, eleven inches tall, tipping the scales at around ninety-five pounds, his butterfly weight a positive asset in what was to become his chosen profession.

Below: *Willie Shoemaker eases Ferdinand into the lead at the Kentucky Derby in 1986. They went on to win. With Shoemaker in the saddle that was always a likely occurrence.*

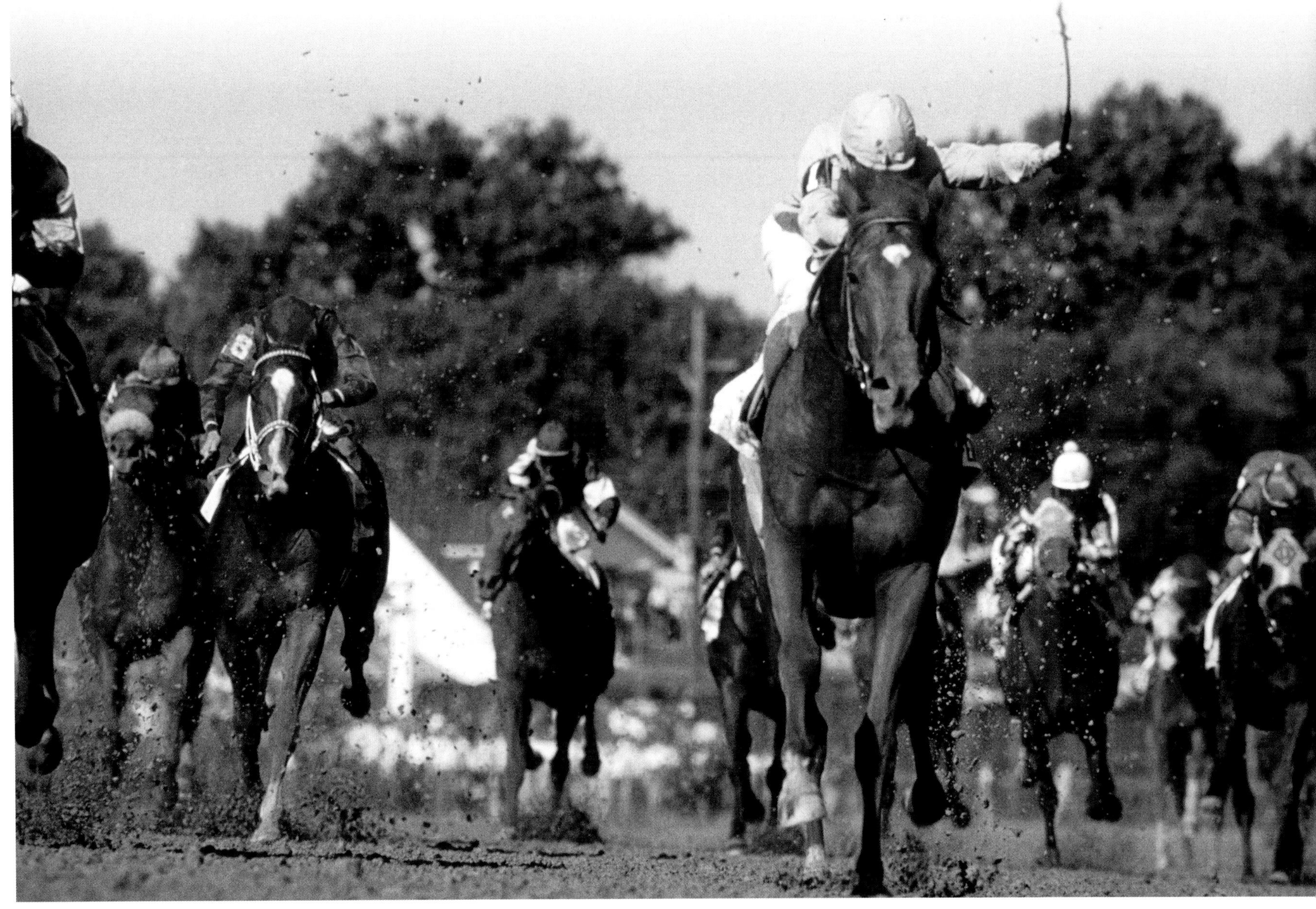

HISTORY IN THE MAKING

Churchill Downs, 1964

The distinctive white blaze of Northern Dancer first saw the light of day in 1961 in Canada. He soon became a compact, good looking horse but the illusion of nobility created a somewhat misleading impression. He was a stable lad's worst nightmare. Indeed, he was virtually unrideable as a newly broken yearling, and consequently failed to reach a reserve of twenty-five thousand dollars when up for sale.

Working in indoor barns during the harsh, long Canadian winters, the horse would regularly barge through the rest of the string, careering headlong into the wooden walls. Fortunately when he became a two-year-old he began to mature and, whilst he remained an undeniable handful, he also began to react to discipline and showed promise on the racetrack. He won five out of his seven races during that first season and the future would have looked promising were it not for the hairline quarter crack that developed on his front hoof. Fortunately a specialist blacksmith was imported and fused the hoofwall with heat treatment.

As a three-year-old he lost a race after his jockey disturbed his highly strung mount with overuse of the whip and so the connections turned to the soft hands and 'cotton fingers' of Bill Shoemaker. The pair won the next two races, including the Florida Derby but when it came to the Kentucky Derby, Shoemaker opted for Hill Rise instead.

So Bill Hartack got the ride instead and piloted Northern Dancer through a tight and closely contested race. So close that Hartack was forced to go for the whip, but this time Northern Dancer was unaffected and indeed showed great guts to win by a neck from Shoemaker and Hill Rise in a record time of two minutes. His record stood until Secretariat won in 1973.

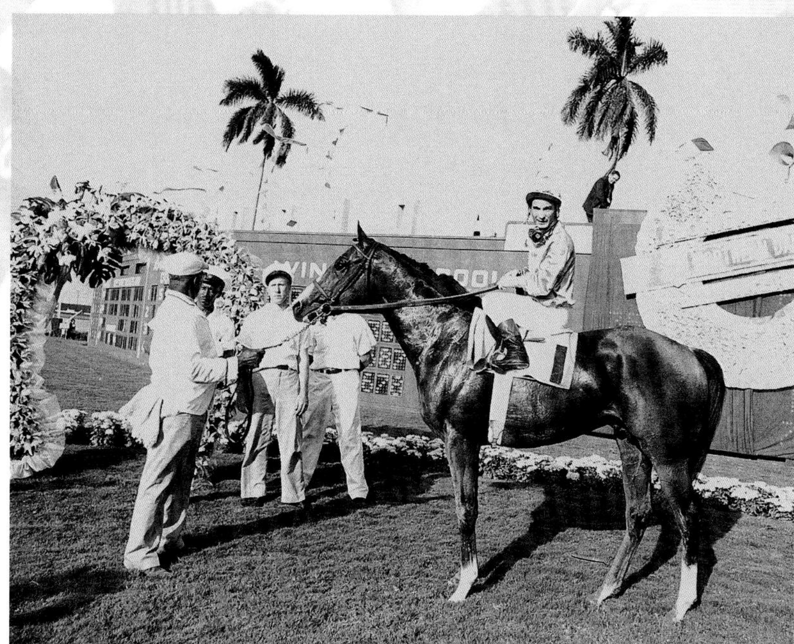

***Right:** Bill Hartack and Northen Dancer in the winner's circle at Gulfstream Park, Hallandale, in April 1964.*

This may have been Northern Dancer's finest hour but there was plenty to come. He also won the Preakness Stakes at Pimlico and although he failed to secure the Triple Crown – his staying power finally wilting – at Belmont, he subsequently won the Queen's Plate.

In all he won fourteen out of eighteen races and was already established as the finest Canadian racehorse – though, nowadays, followers of Nijinsky may have different opinions – before he went to stud and became the most successful thoroughbred sire of the whole twentieth century, across Europe and North America. Nijinsky and Sadler's Wells were among his progeny and at the peak of his powers he warranted eight hundred thousand dollars as a sire. As Robert Sangster once said, "There are two types of stallions – Northern Dancer and the rest". He retired in 1987 and died at the ripe old age of twenty-nine.

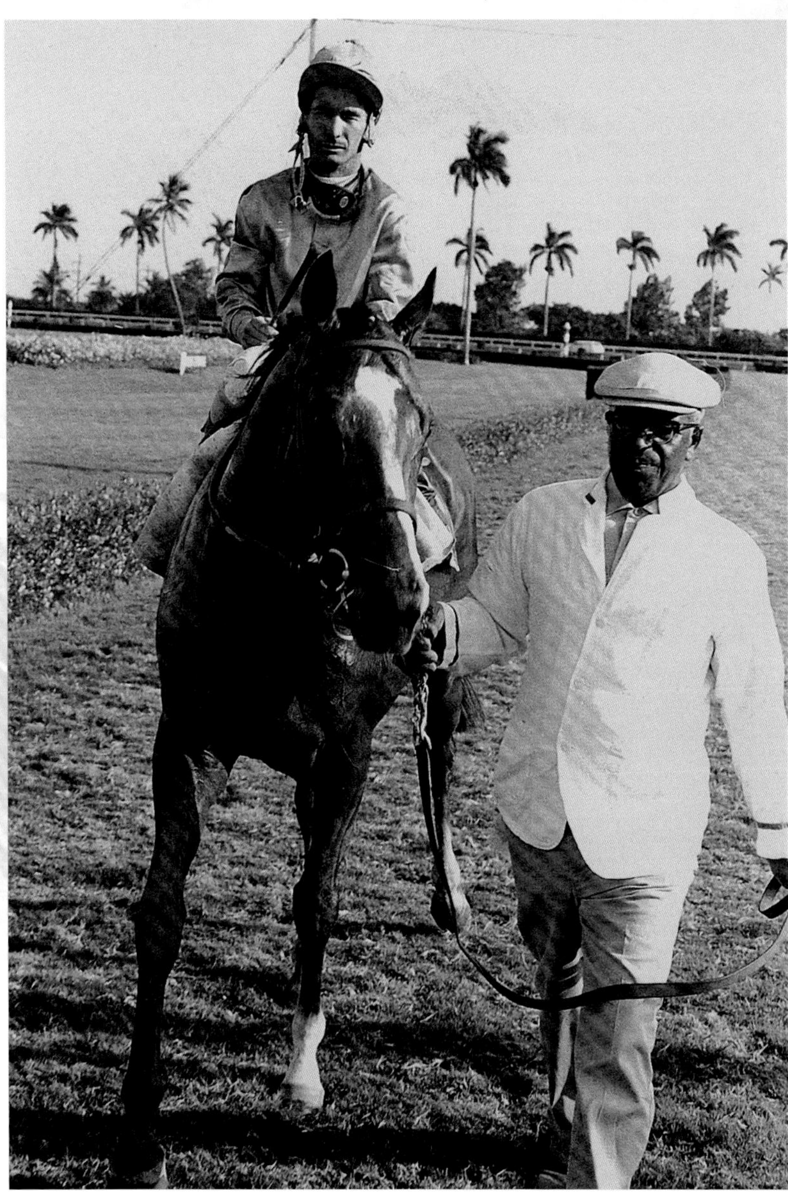

***Right:** Northern Dancer's legacy was not left on the racetracks. He was a stallion who sired some exquisite, turbo-charged thoroughbred racing machines.*

He won eleven Triple Crown races (four Kentucky Derbys, two Preakness Stakes and five Belmont Stakes) though the U.S. Triple Crown proved elusive. At the 1986 Kentucky Derby Shoemaker became the oldest jockey (fifty-four) ever to win the race, aboard outsider Ferdinand. He rode between 1949 and 1990 and amassed a remarkable eight thousand, eight hundred and thirty-three victories. Alas, he was subsequently involved in a car accident which left him paralysed from the neck down and wheelchair-bound.

Donoghue, Richards, Piggott, Breasley, Moore, Arcaro, Shoemaker – these jockeys dominated the first three-quarters of the twentieth century in the same way as Archer and Murphy had dominated the latter part of the one before.

Since then it has proven more difficult to establish quite the same longevity at the top, possibly because the top jockeys chase quality above quantity. The racecourses of Britain, for instance, have hosted fine horsemen, post-Piggott, but none has achieved quite the same degree of prominence.

Above: *Yves St Martin – one of France's finest ever jockeys and a multiple classic winner, both on home soil and in Britain.*

Left: *Walter Swinburn on the great Shergar as they cruise into the history books with a crushing Derby win at Epsom. This was a day when Swinburn had an easy ride.*

These include:

Willie Carson, whose contagious laugh camouflaged a fierce fighting spirit. He was champion jockey five times and won seventeen English classics to boot.

The Frenchman Yves St Martin who won seven classics in England, not to mention twenty-nine on home soil – including four wins in the Prix de l'Arc de Triomphe – where he was champion jockey fifteen times.

Walter Swinburn, a big race rider, who accompanied the great Shergar to his Epsom Derby triumph in 1981.

Ireland's Pat Eddery – four thousand, six hundred and thirty-two winners, three Epsom Derby wins and champion jockey on eleven occasions.

Below: *Even through the goggles, it is possible to sense the desire and concentration of Ireland's Pat Eddery as he drives to another winner, this time at Lingfield in 2003.*

***Above:** Steve Cauthen moves Affirmed (number six) into contention in the Belmont Stakes as the field moves into the home straight. The U.S. Triple Crown is now just seconds away.*

***Left:** To the victors the spoils. Steve Cauthen reviews the silverware after winning the U.S. Triple Crown in June 1978. Cauthen was also successful across the Atlantic.*

American Steve Cauthen, who made his mark on both sides of the Atlantic and became the only man to win the Derbys at Churchill Downs, Epsom, the Curragh and Chantilly. He also rode Affirmed to the U.S. Triple Crown in 1978.

In addition to Cauthen, American racing has enjoyed a strong crop of talent towards the end of the century. None more so than Laffit Pincay Junior from Panama City who surpassed Shoemaker's haul of winners and went on to win more than nine thousand races. His story is of rags to riches since beginning his career at the age of fifteen as an unpaid hot walker.

Others include the volatile and self-assured Angel Cordero Junior from Puerto Rico whose race tactics could test the rulebooks; Colorado-born Pat Day – another firebrand in his youth, but a born-again Christian whose achievements include five wins in the Preakness Stakes; Chris McCarron from Massachusetts, a more thoughtful rider whose prize money surpassed two hundred and forty-seven million dollars; and Dallas-born Jerry Bailey who rode quarter horses in match races aged twelve and overcame personal adversity to join the list of fine and famous race riders.

To split or categorize this group would be difficult but there is certainly little doubt over the finest woman jockey. Michigan's Julie Krone became the first to win a Triple Crown race when she won the Belmont Stakes in 1993 and the first to win a Breeders' Cup race ten years later. A four foot ten inch pocket dynamo, she retired in 2004 with more than three thousand winners in the United States alone.

Below: *Colorado's Pat Day and Louis Quatorze after winning the Preakness Stakes at Pimlico. Day won the Preakness five times in total.*

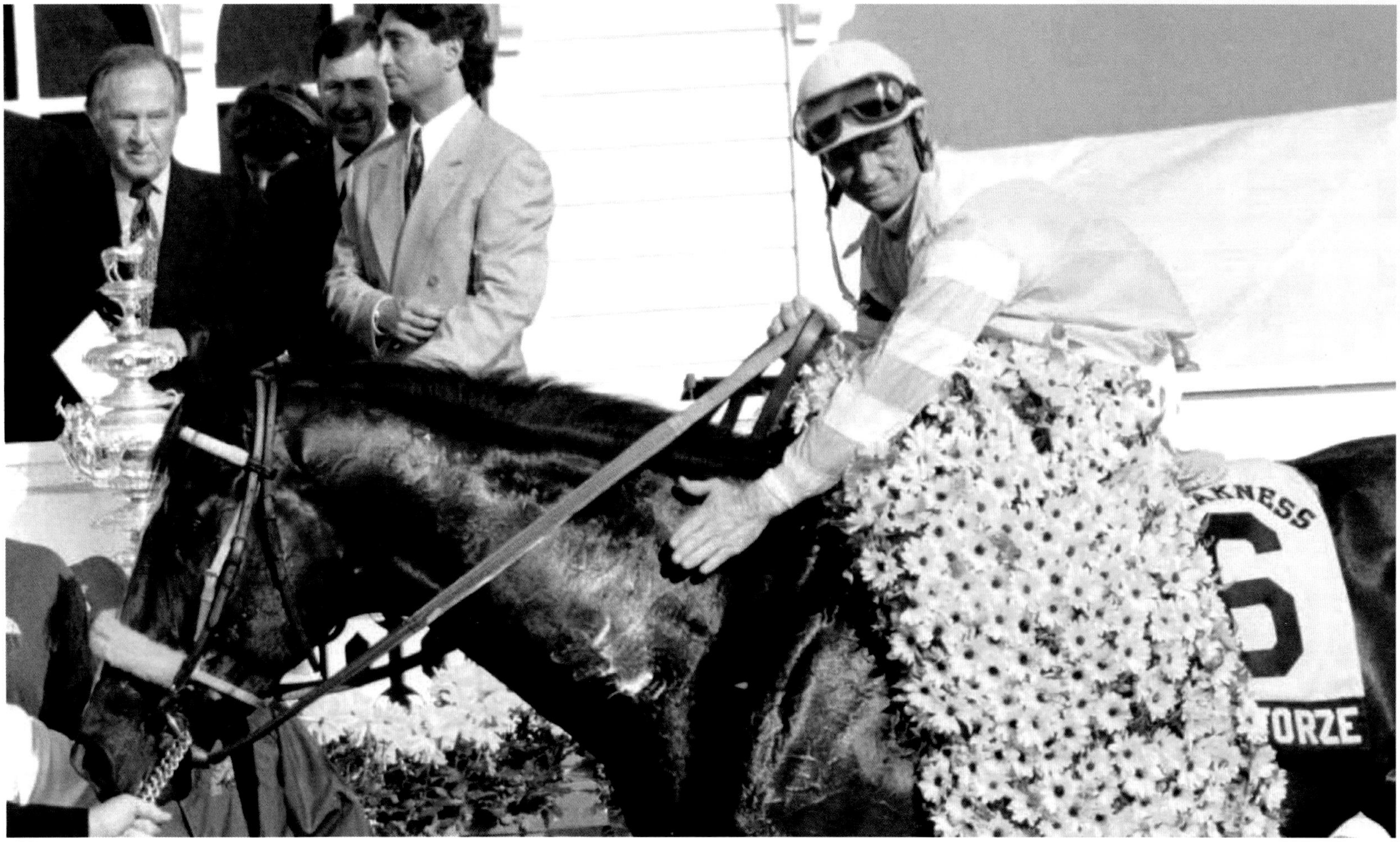

Right: *Affirmed again, this time with Laffit Pincay Jnr on board. The jockey from Panama City beat Willie Shoemaker's record of winners, a feat of skill and resolution.*

***Left:** Julie Krone on Halfbridled (in the blue colours on the left) in action at the 2003 Breeders' Cup World Thoroughbred Championships at Santa Anita. Krone, a tiny but powerful woman, who mixed it with the men and was a trailblazer for female jockeys.*

***Below:** A moment of pure adrenalin when the ceaseless travel, continual wasting and ever-present danger seem small sacrifices to make. Damien Oliver rides Doriemus to victory in the Melbourne Cup in 1995.*

Australia too has had its modern luminaries, including Mick Dittman, known as 'the enforcer' because of a strong, aggressive riding style, and Damien Oliver who twice won the Melbourne Cup, on Doriemus in 1995 and Media Puzzle in 2002. Oliver has also had four victories in the Caulfield Cup, two in the Cox Plate and one in the Golden Slipper.

As the century came to an end, an Irishman, Keiren Fallon, dominated the jockey's title in England for several years, but perhaps the most likely aspirant to join the icons from the golden age was the Italian, Lanfranco Dettori.

Son of a multiple champion jockey, his first winner came at the age of sixteen and he became the first teenager since Piggott to ride one hundred winners in one English season. Further success followed, and in 1996 he won all seven races on the card in a single day at Ascot.

Dettori is one of the new breed, a world traveller in the pursuit of glory in the blue riband events. He is also media-savvy, basking in the limelight, promoting himself and his sport with a ready smile and a quick wit. Despite his six-month ban for a failed drugs test in 2012 and the announced loss of his Godolphin retainer in 2013, Dettori should have no trouble finding rides as a freelancer. The sport, the world, may have changed but the talent, aptitude and courage of its top jockeys remains a constant.

Right: *Frankie Dettori in typically effervescent mood after winning the 2008 Breeders' Cup Classic on Raven's Pass. The Italian is more than comfortable in the limelight, which is just as well as there are few higher profile characters in the sport.*

Below: *Damien Oliver (right) rides Midnight Mustang to victory at the Melbourne Cup meeting in 2008. He was charged in 2012 of betting ten thousand dollars on a rival horse.*

Chapter 7: Racing in Their Blood

On racedays it is the thoroughbreds and their jockeys who take centre stage in the public eye, although the sport is entirely dependent on the patronage of those whose involvement is nearer the shadows. Through their investment, owners provide racecourses with runners and riders, trainers with clients, the media with material and racegoers with a spectacle to watch. The day when they decline to do so will be an ominous one for horse racing.

Fortunately, there appears little immediate prospect of that. If anything, the desire of monarchs, celebrities, aristocrats and well-heeled executives to be associated with racing seems as strong as ever even though common sense and even a fleeting analysis of the laws of probability suggest that the odds are stacked against them making a profit.

Why do they do it? Perhaps it is because the connection between a man's worth and the worth of his horse goes back centuries. In 1250 a knight-farmer wrote to Emperor Frederick II stating, "No animal is more noble than a horse, since it is by horses that Princes, Magnates and Kings are separated from lesser people".

Below: *Queen Elizabeth II with her horse, Aureole, after a win at the Royal Ascot meeting in 1954. The previous year the horse came second to Pinza in the Epsom Derby. The Queen has been a staunch supporter of the sport and is as knowledgeable as she is enthusiastic.*

Certainly the modern-day British royalty retain the same enthusiasm for breeding and horse racing as James I and Charles I and II. Queen Elizabeth II inherited her interest from her father George VI, and when Sir Gordon Richards eventually won his first Epsom Derby, it was her horse, Aureole, who came second. She has owned five classic winners but that was the closest she has got to success at Epsom. Nevertheless, it has not dampened her enthusiasm for the event. She attends every June.

The Queen Mother's preference was for steeplechasing and she did much to raise its profile. In 1956 she nearly won the Grand National with Devon Loch but he inexplicably lost his footing fifty yards from the winning post, and slid to the turf allowing E.S.B. to pass him. Also undeterred by ill fate, the Queen Mother continued to patronise the sport until she passed away.

Others who have invested heavily in the sport during the twentieth century – and have had immense wealth at their disposal to do so – include H.H. Aga Khans III and IV and Robert Sangster.

H.H. Aga Khan III dominated racing ownership in the 1930s when he built an unprecedented team of horses and studs. The benefits of his work included seventeen classic victories, including Bahram, who won the English Triple Crown in 1935.

Left: *H.H. Aga Khan III leads in Bahram after the 1935 Epsom Derby. Bahram won the English Triple Crown that year, one of many successes for the owner.*

HISTORY IN THE MAKING
Longchamp, 1965

Ribot's double success at Longchamp, along with an impressive sixteen-run unbeaten record, established his credentials as a thoroughbred of high class. But few promote him as the horse of the century. Perhaps that accolade should be assigned to Man o' War? Or maybe Secretariat? All up for debate of course, but many Europeans would advance the cause of Sea-Bird, a winner at Longchamp nine years after Ribot's finest hour.

A chestnut with a white blaze and two white stockings the French Sea-Bird came from dubious pedigree. On his dam's side not one of the female forebears had ever won a race. Yet even though the tall, rangy colt was an unexceptional two-year-old, his performances as a three-year-old were singular.

Firstly he won the 1965 Epsom Derby with absurd ease. Perfectly poised in sixth at Tattenham Corner, each long and graceful stride down the home straight eased him past a field of Europe's twenty best three-year-olds. He actually only won by two lengths, but that was a misleading statistic as the horse never came off the bridle and his jockey, Pat Glennon, employed cruise control. If need be, he could have won by ten times more.

Yet, in fact, that 'once in a lifetime performance' was bettered later that same year when he claimed the Prix de l'Arc de Triomphe on home soil at Longchamp with the most awe-inspiring masterpiece.

For Sea-Bird to win it at all was a notable achievement. To win in such style underlined that this was a horse of rare distinction.

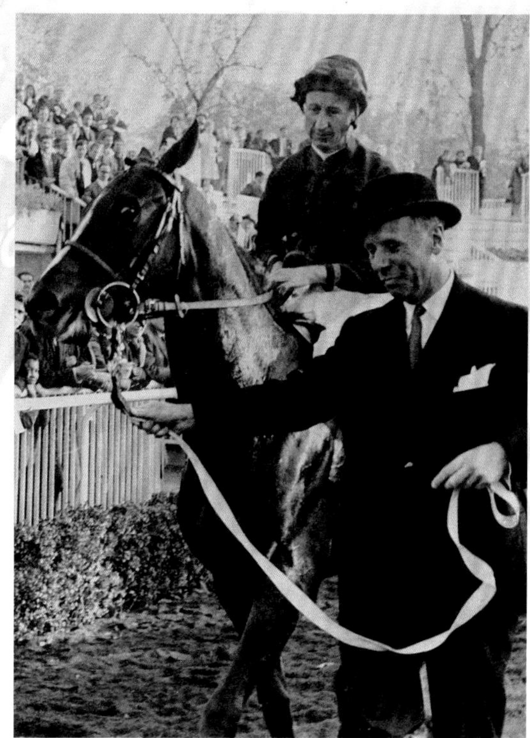

Right: *The 4th October 1965. A memorable day for the French and all those who love top-class sporting action. Jean Ternynck leads in Sea-Bird after the Prix de l'Arc de Triomphe.*

Ironically, there was little indication of what was to come from Sea-Bird's pre-race demeanour. His powerful chestnut quarters became soaked in sweat in the October sunshine. He was on the edge, burning energy that it seemed he could ill afford considering the quality of the opposition also circling in the parade ring. There was Reliance II and Diatome, winner and runner-up in the French Derby; the Russian champion, Anilin; Meadow Court, runner-up in the Epsom Derby; and the Preakness Stakes winner from America, Tom Rolfe. To win, Sea-Bird would have to defeat the crème de la crème.

It was the Russian, Anilin, who held the advantage as the field entered the home straight, but, as with the Epsom Derby, Sea-Bird was poised. He then kicked, swept by and although Reliance II threatened briefly, Sea-Bird found another gear and established a five-length lead in the blink of an eye. Although he veered diagonally across the track in the last furlong, he still won by six lengths.

Sea-Bird's greatness was perhaps best summed up by sportswriter Frank Keating who wrote that the horse "won the great Epsom classic with such contemptuous ease that jockey Pat Glennon dropped his hands eighty yards from the pole and they almost trotted past the line … three months later the sumptuously haughty chestnut with the two white stockings behind did exactly the same back home in the Prix de l'Arc de Triomphe. On both occasions you knew no other horse in the world could have beaten him – indeed no other horse in the century."

Above: *Sea-Bird is again welcomed into the winning enclosure, this time at Epsom after his afternoon stroll into the history books.*

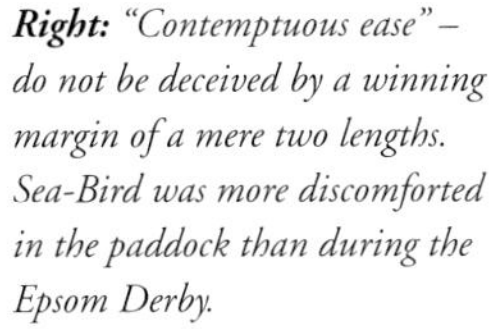

Right: *"Contemptuous ease" – do not be deceived by a winning margin of a mere two lengths. Sea-Bird was more discomforted in the paddock than during the Epsom Derby.*

Below: *H.H. Aga Khan IV (right) after Zarkasa won the 2008 Prix de l'Arc de Triomphe at Longchamp. He operates a large horse racing and breeding operation in France.*

His grandson, H.H. Aga Khan IV's prime time was towards the end of the century, illuminating European racing with Epsom Derby winners Shergar (1981), Shahrastani (1986), Kahyasi (1988) and Sinndar (2000). He became the leading owner in Britain in 1981 and 2000, and went on to operate the largest horse racing and breeding operation in France, four kilometres from Chantilly racecourse, underlining a philosophy that prefers the production of home-bred talent above purchases at bloodstock auctions. In 2008 he won the Prix de l'Arc de Triomphe with the filly, Zarkava.

The flamboyant, multimillionaire Robert Sangster first got involved in horse racing ownership as a twenty-four-year-old, and he owned some of the best horses of his generation in The Minstrel, Alleged, Detroit, Beldale Ball and Sadler's Wells.

Five-time champion owner and twice a winner at the Epsom Derby, Sangster created a racing and breeding empire with interests in England, Australia, Venezuela, the United States of America, Ireland, France and New Zealand. Sangster recognized the commercial value of stallions and followed a strategy to produce champions on the track that could also become major stallions in racing retirement.

Although his emerald green and royal blue colours were constantly seen in winners' enclosures, perhaps his most far-reaching contribution to racing was to help establish the Coolmore operation with John Magnier and Vincent O'Brien in the 1970s.

O'Brien underlined this achievement when he paid tribute to Sangster after his death in 2004: "Robert was a true visionary whose large-scale investment in the best American-bred yearlings in the seventies was one of the principal factors in establishing Ireland and Coolmore as major forces in the bloodstock world. His knowledge of bloodstock was extensive and professional, and it was helpful to get his opinion on all aspects of horse management, training and breeding."

Associations in racing are common. Owners build trust with certain trainers, and trainers have favoured jockeys. Sometimes those relationships are formalized, sometimes not, but when wealthy, ambitious owners join forces with talented trainers and jockeys then success tends to follow. So when a deep-pocketed owner like Sangster joined forces with a trainer as good as O'Brien and a jockey as good as Lester Piggott then the result was a racing certainty.

__Right:__ Robert Sangster: a flamboyant visionary and also immensely knowledgeable. He was an adept talent-spotter of bloodstock.

__Below:__ Vincent O'Brien leads in Nijinsky after the 1970 Epsom Derby win, Lester Piggott on board. One of O'Brien's many gifts was to time and tailor his training so that the likes of Nijinsky peaked on raceday.

HISTORY IN THE MAKING

Aintree, 1967

Foinavon was owned by Anne, Duchess of Westminster, and trained by Tom Dreaper in Ireland, one of the great trainers. But even Dreaper could do little with him. Yes, he had a semblance of ability but his attitude would drive the most laid-back of trainers to distraction.

In a chase at Balydoyle he fell when in the lead at the third last and lay prostrate for ages. His concerned connections rushed over to him, only to find him on his feet and picking at the grass around him. He was sold by the frustrated Duchess for two thousand guineas and came to be trained by John Kempton.

Foinavon was often entered for the big races but he never actually featured at the end of the contest. He was an also-ran with no prospect of improvement. In 1967 he was last home in the Cheltenham Gold Cup, no surprise considering his odds of five hundred to one.

So, little money had been placed on his head for the Grand National at Aintree a month or so later. A similar result was anticipated with the view that any horse that finished behind him – assuming Foinavon actually finished at all – would have run very poorly. Indeed, the chances of him actually completing the gruelling four and a half miles appeared microscopically minute.

So it was a minor triumph that jockey and horse were still together as the cavalry charge jumped Becher's Brook on Aintree's second circuit. Still together, but barely visible, so far were they behind the race leaders who were accompanied, significantly as it turned out, by one Popham Down, a loose horse who had parted company with his jockey earlier in the race but was still intent on completing the course.

Right: *The leaders at Becher's Brook. Foinavon is most definitely not in the picture. It was a while before he reached the obstacle.*

That intention remained until the smallest fence on the course, fence twenty-three, when Popham Down not only decided he had had enough of racing for the day and refused to jump the fence, but ran directly across the take-off ground. Havoc ensued. All the front runners were brought to a standstill and the second wave of combatants cannoned into them. Not one of the group who retained a realistic chance of success in the race managed to jump the fence. All were caught up in the biggest and most celebrated equine traffic jam in history.

And then, of course, there was Foinavon, plodding along at the rear of the field. Slowly, as the horse and his rider, John Buckingham, approached the fence, the chaos could be seen in sharper focus – and Buckingham, to his immense credit, spied a gap. Sure enough he navigated Foinavon through the carnage and over the fence and set off for home as a legion of unseated jockeys tried to locate their horses and remount. By the time the race's favourite, Honey End, set off in pursuit it was too late. Foinavon somehow managed to negotiate the remaining fences and won the historic race by fifteen lengths.

Of course the fence was named after him. Of course there has never been another Grand National like it. And the name of Foinavon, to everyone's surprise including – you would surmise – his own, had entered racing folklore.

***Above Right:** The biggest and most celebrated equine traffic jam in history. Only John Buckingham and Foinavon managed to tip-toe around the multitude of obstacles.*

***Right:** By now many have remounted, but too late to catch the one hundred to one outsider.*

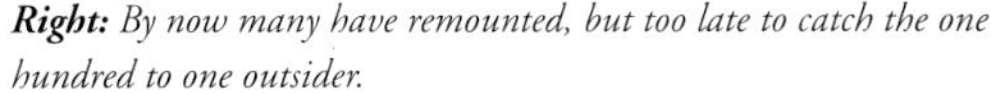

Yet if it is owners who hold the purse strings and the power within racing, it is the trainers who are treated with the greater reverence and acclaim, mainly for what is seen as an almost mystical power to convert raw thoroughbred potential into money-earning headline makers, both on the racecourse and at stud.

Vincent O'Brien was perhaps one of the best in this regard. He was an adroit talent-spotter, expert at identifying yearlings with high-class pedigrees that would perform well on the track and at stud. Then he understood their quirks and foibles, recognizing that, like humans, each thoroughbred has its own character.

Equally, O'Brien recognized that each has a singular tolerance to exercise. Some thrive on regular 'work' and racing, others respond to a lighter workload with long periods of recovery and recuperation. Most train in cycles, building to a peak that can only be maintained for a short period. O'Brien was also ahead of his time in recognizing the need for effective nutrition, importing the best Canadian oats for example. If thoroughbreds are just one per cent from their peak then that can be the difference between a race won and a race lost. More than most, O'Brien timed and tailored his training so that his horses peaked on the racecourse, and he earned suitable acclaim from peers and punters as a result.

What is more admirable still is that he demonstrated this uncanny knack both over the jumps and on the flat. Through the 1940s and 1950s he made a name for himself in the winter game with three consecutive Cheltenham Gold Cups (1948, 1949 and 1950), Champion Hurdles (1949, 1950 and 1951) and Grand Nationals (1953, 1954 and 1955). He was the top steeplechase trainer of his generation and achieved all that there was to achieve. So what did he do? He turned his attention to flat racing, an unusual and imaginative gamble.

If anything he became even more successful here, racking up sixteen English classics (six wins in the Epsom Derby), twenty-seven Irish classics, twenty-five wins at Royal Ascot, three Prix de l'Arc de Triomphes and a Breeders' Cup.

__Below:__ Australian, Bart Cummings at Flemington. Cummings's record at the Melbourne Cup is the stuff of dreams. Here he is holding the Cup with winner number twelve, viewed in 2008.

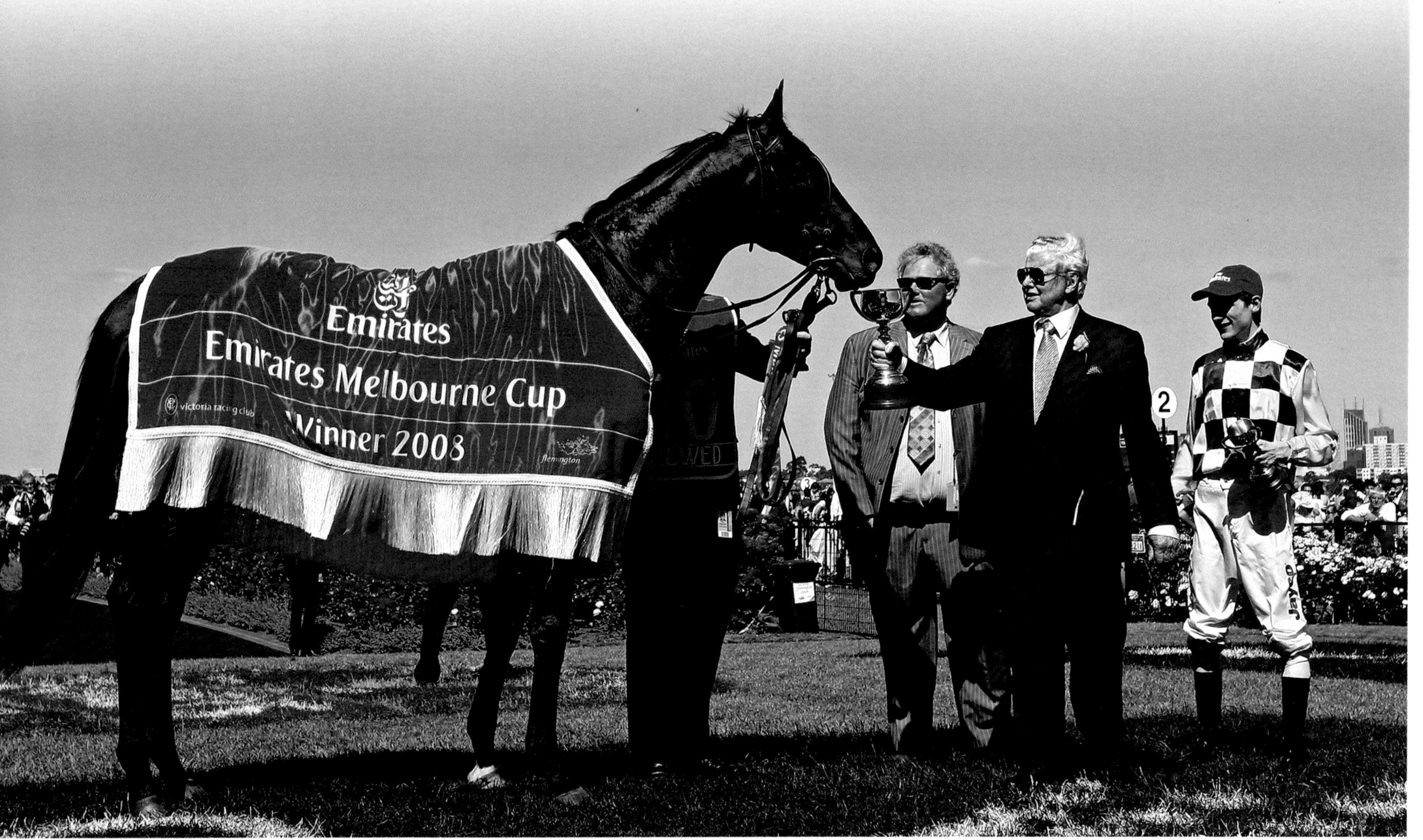

Nevertheless, despite this record, O'Brien should not sit alone on his pedestal. There have been other trainers who have demonstrated similar gifts, employed similar methods and enjoyed similar success; two of them from Australia.

Tommy Smith, born one year after O'Brien, won more than seven thousand races, and for thirty-three seasons headed the trainers' premiership in Sydney. On the national stage he won the Melbourne Cup twice with Toporosa in 1955 and Just a Dash in 1981. Perhaps he was even more indebted to Tulloch who won thirty-six out of fifty-three races in the 1950s and Kingston Town who won thirty out of forty-one, including a hat-trick of success in the Cox Plate in 1980, 1981 and 1982.

James Bartholomew – better known as 'Bart' – Cummings had racing in his blood. His father, Jim, was a successful trainer in his own right and 'Bart' followed suit, receiving his trainer licence in 1953 and initially setting up stables in South Australia.

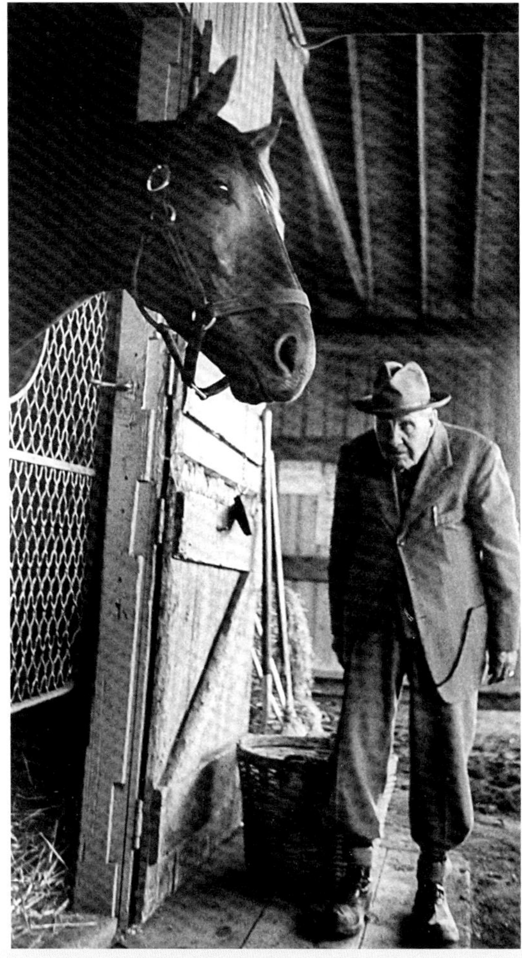

***Right:** 'Sunny Jim' Fitzsimmons. To his name: two U.S. Triple Crowns, with Gallant Fox and Omaha, and a total of thirteen Triple Crown events.*

***Left:** D. Wayne Lukas escorts Charismatic prior to the Preakness Stakes in 1999. Lukas says he does nothing but work and has no balance in his life, but eighteen wins at the Breeders' Cup must help to make it worthwhile.*

In 1965, 1966 and 1967 he trained a trio of Melbourne Cup winners – Light Fingers, Galilee and Red Handed. And in 1969 he had high hopes for the pre-race favourite, Big Philou, who had already won the Caulfield Cup. However, the horse was drugged with laxatives on the eve of the race and had to withdraw. This must have driven him to despair. Even without such treachery, thoroughbreds are quite susceptible enough to muscle tears, pulls and strains, viruses, inflammations, infections, abscesses and internal bleeding to name just a few from a depressingly long list. As U.S. trainer, Bobby Frankel once explained, "You get a horse ready for a race and they start coughing, they bleed, they lose a shoe. The public doesn't know that. They only lose their money, not their minds."

However, Cummings's disappointment might have been assuaged if he had known the success that would continue in the future at Flemington. So far he has won no less than twelve Melbourne Cups in total – and in 1965, 1966, 1974, 1975 and 1991 he trained horses that finished in both first and second place. Despite the last-minute drama surrounding Big Philou, Cummings cherished the race and it was kind to him in return. The two have become synonymous and he won yet again in 2008 with Viewed.

America, too, can boast some illustrious trainers, including 'Sunny Jim' Fitzsimmons, born in 1874. He trained Gallant Fox and Omaha to Triple Crowns and, in all, won three Kentucky Derbys, four Preakness Stakes and six Belmont Stakes – a record of thirteen Triple Crown events that has only been equalled by D. (Darren) Wayne Lukas.

Born in Wisconsin in 1935, Lukas graduated from university with a master's degree in education and taught at high school for nine years where he was head basketball coach. Yet the interest in horses that had first surfaced as he grew up on a small farm led him to begin to train quarter horses in California at the age of thirty-three. He was good. During a decade of achievement he trained twenty-three world champions, before he switched to thoroughbreds with similar success. The first trainer to earn more than one hundred million dollars in purse money, he has topped the money list fourteen times.

His horses have won the Kentucky Derby and Belmont Stakes (both four times) and the Preakness Stakes (five). This included a clean sweep of the Triple Crown in 1995 with Thunder Gulch (at Churchill Downs and Belmont Stakes) and Timber Country (Pimlico) that sat in the middle of a run of six successive Triple Crown successes. In 1994 Tabasco Cat had won the last two legs, and in 1996 Grindstone made it six out of six when he won the Kentucky Derby.

In addition, his eighteen Breeders' Cup wins are unsurpassed. But, in line with other trainers Lukas has recognized that his glorious obsession has side effects. "I'm a sick person," he once said, "I do nothing but work. I have no balance in my life and I recognize that. I've gone through numerous marriages because the horses are always a priority and I don't think that makes for a good marriage, and I'll admit that openly."

***Above:** English trainer Sir Henry Cecil at Royal Ascot. Cecil has been a successful trainer for decades. His most notable skill was with fillies.*

***Left:** Light Shift (number eight) wins the 2007 Oaks for Henry Cecil. This was a particularly emotional win for the trainer as it followed a fight against cancer and some comparatively fallow years.*

Across the Atlantic, someone – who has suffered more than his share of vicissitudes but remains a racing man to his core – has carried O'Brien's baton: Sir Henry Cecil. Born a twin during the Second World War, Cecil's father was killed in action in North Africa. His widowed mother married Cecil Boyd-Rochfort and he became an assistant trainer there in 1964.

Leading trainer in England on ten occasions, Cecil enjoyed some halcyon years. He won the Derby and St Leger four times and the Two Thousand Guineas three times, but he was particularly adept at preparing fillies. "I think you've got to take them very gently, rather like women!" he once quipped. He won the One Thousand Guineas six times, the Oaks eight times and trained Oh So Sharp to the fillies' Triple Crown in 1985.

Right: *A joyous beam from Sir Michael Stoute – and little wonder. Stoute has competed, toe to toe and with considerable success with major breeding and training operations like Godolphin and Coolmore.*

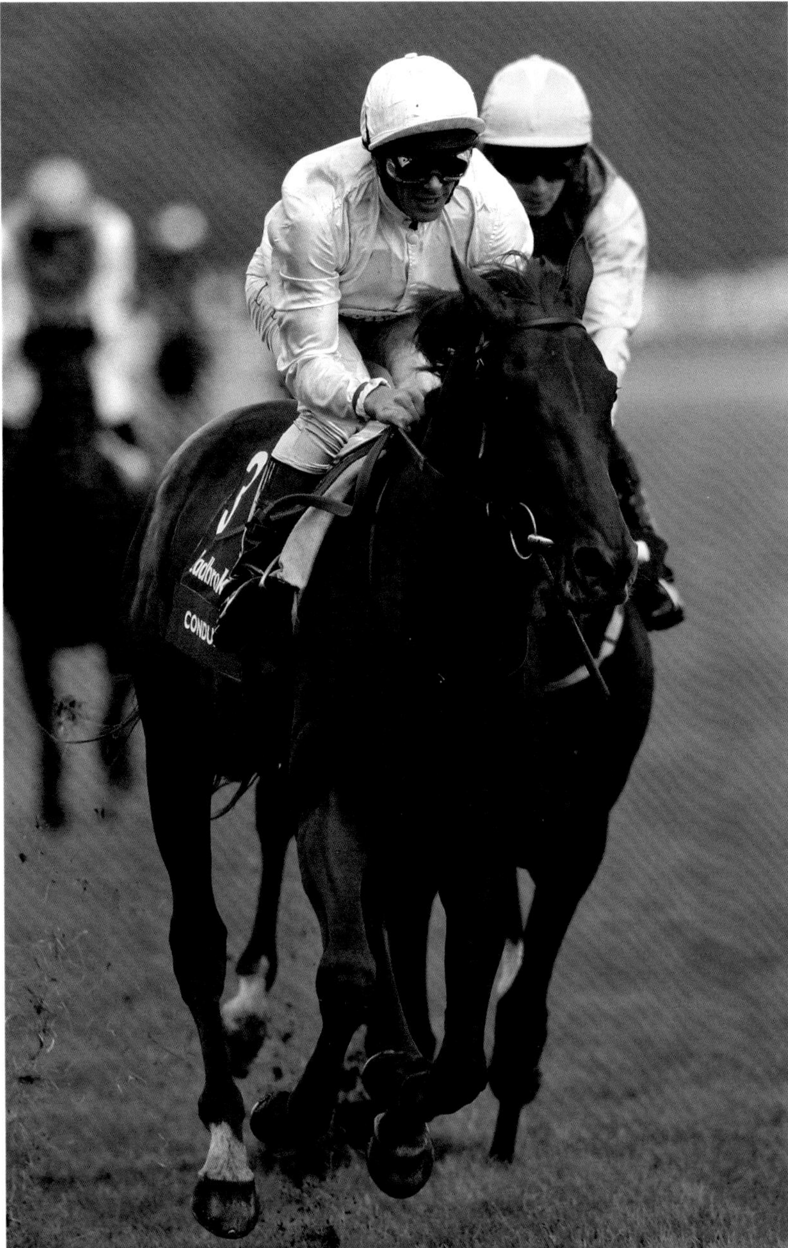

After each big win the family standard (depicting the Horn of Leys, an heirloom given to one of Cecil's ancestors by Robert the Bruce in 1323) was raised outside his stables in Newmarket. It was a familiar sight – until famine followed feast. Cecil suffered that most cruel but basic of trainer ailments: he went out of favour. No flying of the standard. Fewer owners. Fewer horses. "I used to think that if anyone wanted a horse trained by me they would ring up and ask, and that if I had to ask anyone to train their horse they probably weren't the people I wanted to have as owners," he said in 2000. "But I haven't had many people ringing me up recently."

Cecil also suffered from stomach cancer, so his rehabilitation and renaissance in fortunes (featuring that eighth win in the Oaks with Light Shift in 2007, and his best season for a decade in 2011 thanks to the unbeaten Frankel, whose wins included Cecil's third Two Thousand Guineas that year – 25 years after his last win) was received warmly by an appreciative public. He received his knighthood for services to horse racing in 2011.

Perhaps Cecil's most regular combatant during his heyday was Sir Michael Stoute, another trainer based in Newmarket. Stoute had been born in Barbados, where his father was Chief of Police, and in 1998 was knighted for services to tourism. However, he moved to England at the age of nineteen and demonstrated that his primary expertise – some have labelled it genius – was in training racehorses as he established a record comparable with the best, preparing some of the generation's top horses such as Shergar, Pilsudski and Singspiel.

Champion trainer ten times, his long-awaited St Leger win in 2008, at the twenty-sixth attempt, meant that the last of the English classics had fallen to his masterly touch.

Left: *Twenty-sixth time lucky. Sir Michael Stoute's outstanding record as a trainer had one blot; he had never won the St Leger. But Conduit (in the white colours) put the record straight in 2008.*

HISTORY IN THE MAKING
Royal Ascot, 1975

The 26th of July 1975 was a hot summer's day in England. Vast crowds enjoyed the heat wave at Royal Ascot, perspiring lightly (the upper classes never sweat) in their top hats and tails and their extravagant and ludicrously expensive dresses. The rich and the royals, and the beautiful. Champagne and lobster. A social scene par excellence – and racing of the highest order, fit for both the occasion and the blissful weather.

The King George VI and Queen Elizabeth Diamond Stakes is always one of the highlights of the Royal Ascot Festival. It was particularly worthy of attention in 1975 because of the delicious prospect of a head-to-head between two outstanding thoroughbreds: Grundy and Bustino.

Grundy cost just eleven thousand guineas as a yearling but had won four out of four as a two-year-old and had claimed the Epsom Derby a couple of months earlier. Bustino, a year older, had won the St Leger in 1974 and represented Grundy's greatest threat in the race.

Sure enough, the contest became an absorbing tactical battle, albeit conducted at breakneck speed. Bustino's trainer, Major Dick Hern, wanted to test Grundy by forcing the pace in the early stages and employed not one but two pacemakers.

Inevitably the straining field became strung out and as they raced into the last half mile the pacemaker moved over and made way for Bustino to move into a four-length advantage as they entered the home straight. However, Grundy, expertly ridden by Pat Eddery, had not been fatigued by the frenetic pace.

Right: *Grundy and Bustino at full stretch as they approach the finishing post. Both horses sustained a remarkable, lung-bursting pace that they were not able to subsequently repeat.*

As they entered the final furlong the two were stride for stride. Grundy nosed ahead, a seemingly decisive lung-bursting injection of speed, but Bustino showed great courage and fought back into contention. As they reached the winning post Grundy inched ahead by half a length, creating a new course record in the process.

It had been a battle royal over one and a half miles, where the pace had never dropped. Both horses had galloped themselves to the edge of exhaustion and were barely able to make it back to the winner's enclosure, never mind repeat the effort in the future.

Bustino's jockey, Joe Mercer, said: "My horse never ran again because he broke down in the race, and without it I think we would probably have won it. Until Grundy got to us inside the distance I think he had the race won, but then he changed his legs, lost a bit of momentum, and Grundy got up to wear him down. But it was a great race; the viewers and spectators loved it and they were two great horses."

Certainly the horse racing aficionados at Royal Ascot went back to their socializing in the sure knowledge that they had seen one of the finest races of all. Indeed, many, at least in Great Britain, considered it to be the race of the century.

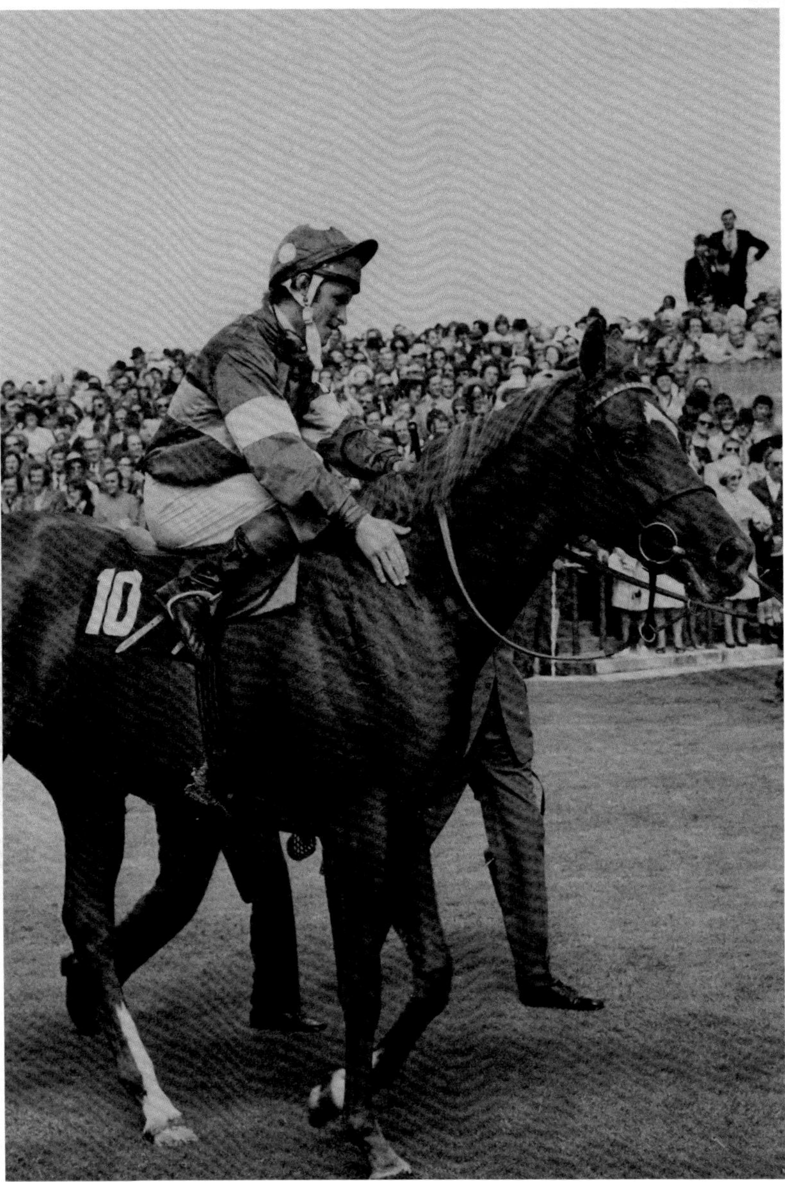

***Right:** Grundy and jockey Pat Eddery receive Ascot's acclaim after their close-fought victory.*

Chapter 8: "His feet would fly"

Jump racing takes two main forms: 'steeplechasing' or 'National Hunt', which is run over distances between two and four and a half miles over fences at least four and a half feet high, and 'hurdling', over distances of between two and three and a half miles over hurdles at least three and a half feet high. Whilst the most widespread form of horse racing is undeniably on the flat, steeplechasing is also prospering in several countries.

In America the Maryland Hunt Cup poses a challenge to horse and rider of twenty-two obstacles of vertical posts and rails over four miles of undulating terrain. Two winners of the race, Ben Nevis II and Jay Trump have gone on to win the Grand National in England. In Japan they have the Nakayama Grand Jump which is run every April at Nakayama racecourse over a winding path on the inside of the oval for just over two and a half miles. And races over jumps are staged annually at more than one hundred and thirty venues in France, most notably in Auteuil in Paris, whose obstacles include 'Le Bullfinch' – a rail, ditch and fence on top of a stone wall. Italy, Australia and Canada are other countries where steeplechasing is enjoyed, but its undeniable hub is in Great Britain and Ireland.

Below: *Ben Nevis II (number six in fourth place), ridden by jockey Charlie Fenwick, negotiates the Water Jump at Aintree in the 1980 Grand National. Ben Nevis went on to win, thereby securing a notable double. He had also won the Maryland Hunt Cup across the Atlantic.*

Here, as the flat racing season winds down with the onset of winter, jump racing comes to the fore. The season gathers momentum, culminating in two celebrated festivals where the elite horses do battle. The first takes place in March at Cheltenham, jump racing's equivalent of Royal Ascot because of its series of world-class races. The second is April's Grand National meeting at Aintree. Millions watch, either at the racecourse or on television, and they gamble millions of pounds.

Certainly, every year owners, breeders, trainers and horse racing fans travel in huge numbers to Cheltenham, intent on success and a good time (the carousing is legendary). Racegoers all have their favourites, and because National Hunt horses tend to be geldings (and so have no breeding value) they race longer and stay in the public affection for longer. They have more time to create a following compared to their 'here today, gone tomorrow' equivalents in the summer game.

An example of this was Golden Miller, still the only horse to have won both the Cheltenham Gold Cup and the Grand National in the same year, a feat he achieved in 1934.

That win was one of five in the Cheltenham Gold Cup, providing joy to his owner, Dorothy Paget – an extraordinary woman, incidentally, who had inherited a fortune, gambled to excess and who was extremely eccentric. Bizarrely, she tended to eat her main meal in the morning, before retiring to bed during daylight and rising for breakfast just before dusk. During the night, she ate and disturbed the slumbers of her trainers with phone calls.

__Above:__ Miss Dorothy Paget, a great British eccentric. There have been many interesting characters inhabiting the world of steeplechasing, but Miss Paget was in a class of her own. Here she leads in Golden Miller after victory in the 1934 Grand National.

__Left:__ Golden Miller pops over another fence – the only horse to win both the Cheltenham Gold Cup and the Grand National in the same season, 1934.

Not all of those involved with steeplechasing have been quite as unconventional as Paget, but many others have fallen under its spell. As an illustration, we need look no further than a Fulke and two Freds. Fulke Walwyn, Fred Rimell and Fred Winter to be precise. All genuine racing folk to their core, who have devoted their lives to jump racing, both as jockeys and trainers.

Fulke Walwyn, marginally the oldest of this band of brothers, was born in 1910 and began riding whilst with the Ninth Lancers on National Service. He won the 1936 Grand National on Reynoldstown. He fractured his skull in 1938 and was unconscious for a whole month, but recovered to be leading trainer in the three years just after the Second World War, and five times in total. From 1973 he trained for the Queen Mother.

Fred Rimell was born three years after Walwyn but was an early developer. He rode his first winner at the age of twelve and went on to be champion jockey four times, even though he twice broke his neck in 1947. As a trainer he won every major race, was leading trainer five times and won four Grand Nationals. In all, his professional association with jump racing spanned more than fifty years.

Fred Winter was born in 1926 and was also a four-time champion jockey, racking up nine hundred winners in total. As a trainer he won eight championships, his dominance most apparent at the beginning of the 1970s. He is the only man to have both ridden and trained the winners of the Grand National, the Gold Cup and the Champion Hurdle.

Above: *National Hunt jockey Fred Winter on Safron Tartan, taking the last fence of the Cheltenham Gold Cup in March 1961, which he went on to win.*

Right: *The 1936 Grand National. Reynoldstown makes hard work of Aintree's water jump. No matter, he went on to win, ridden by Fulke Walwyn, who also went on to enjoy success as a trainer.*

And so it goes on. More recently, John Francome rode for Winter for fifteen unbroken years – though unbroken is always an unfortunate term to apply to a jump jockey. He was a seven-time champion and rode one thousand, one hundred and thirty-eight winners, a mountainous record that was eclipsed by Peter Scudamore, the stable jockey for the stand-out trainer of the modern day: Martin Pipe. He was the most scientific and professional of Englishmen, and was leading trainer for ten consecutive seasons beginning in 1995–6.

Of course, winter brings softer ground, which is just as well as jump jockeys know that they will fall regularly, and that serious injury is not so much a threat as an inevitability. All those who have ridden over several years have broken bones. Not one who has enjoyed a lengthy career has escaped without a body blemished by breaks and dislocations – each one accompanied by its own anecdote. They are, by definition, courageous bordering on crazy.

As English sportswriter, Ian Wooldridge, once wrote, "Like matadors they take their lives in their hands every time they ride. They smash collarbones, arms, legs and vertebrae round the clock and are back in the saddle when most of us would be taking tentative steps on a Zimmer frame. Jump jockeys for me remain the bravest of all our sportsmen."

Above: *The thrill of the chase where falls are inevitable and broken bones an occupational hazard. It is a strange but seemingly compelling way of making a living.*

Left: *Horse and rider in perfect balance and symmetry. John Francome rides Musso over a water jump in 1983. Francome was a supreme jockey, a master in the saddle and a seven-time champion.*

HISTORY IN THE MAKING

Aintree, 1981

It was towards the end of the chemotherapy that Bob Champion felt furthest away from the dream that had kept his spirit and sanity intact. It had been a brutal if necessary regime. Powerful medication had been pumped through his bloodstream to destroy the testicular cancer that threatened not just the thirty-one-year-old's livelihood but his very existence. By then he was weak. His hair had fallen out in clumps, his skin was grey, and the medics could not guarantee that the treatment would provide a cure.

Moreover, the racehorse upon which his dream depended was lame. Tendon trouble had put him out of training. His legs were frail. Would he ever race again? The prospects were at best questionable.

Still, the absurd, impossible dream gave the jockey hope. These were dark, dark days; however, it is sometimes said that it is darkest just before the dawn.

Fast forward just over a year to April 1981. A sun-blessed spring day. The Grand National field is coming 'under starter's orders' at Aintree racecourse. The cavalry charge is about to begin. And, there, lining up, is human and equine evidence that dreams can come true.

In the white and dark blue colours is the jockey, Bob Champion, who had completed the chemotherapy and gradually regained strength and spark. He began to ride again on the flat in America and through expertise, pluck, sheer bloody-mindedness and the help of friends, such as the trainer Josh Gifford, gradually rebuilt his rudely interrupted career.

Under him is the horse that he had earmarked as a potential 'National' horse, Aldaniti. He, too, had made an unlikely recovery and had regained vigour and force.

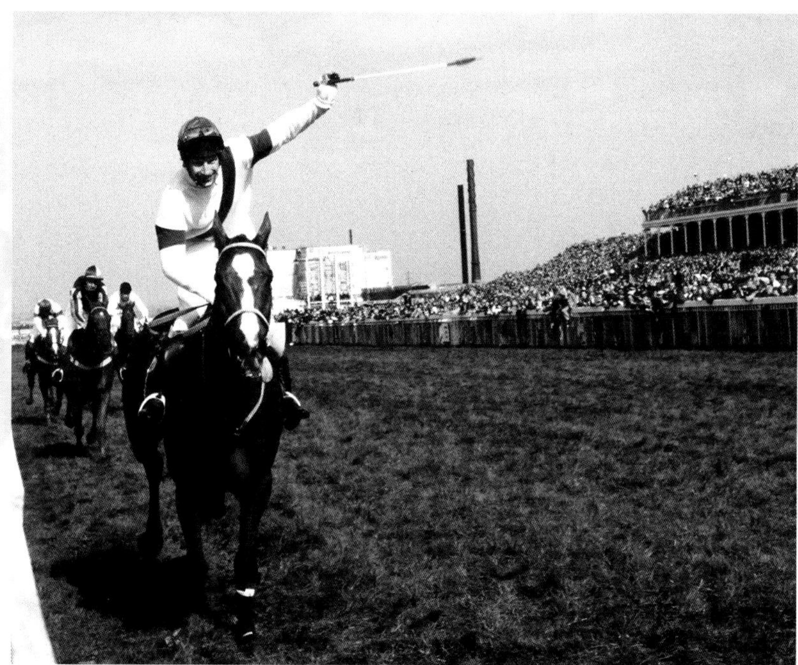

Above: *Dreams do come true. Bob Champion's arm is raised in triumph as Aldaniti wins the 1981 Grand National.*

__Right:__ Aldaniti nearly fell at the first in the 1981 Grand National (indeed he did so in 1982), but thereafter his jumping was flawless.

__Above:__ Aldaniti and Bob Champion. Against mountainous odds, their heroic actions 'wrote' a script worthy of Hollywood.

The historic race, by its very nature, has always had an uncanny ability to churn out stories that continue to embroider the legend. The fact that Bob Champion and Aldaniti were amongst those lining up at the start of the Grand National – indeed rated by bookmakers as an eight to one shot – did just that. But even by Aintree standards, what happened next was pure Hollywood.

At the first fence Aldaniti jumped like a novice, paddled his feet on the floor, but survived. He also barely jumped the second. Thereafter, though, he was faultless, inspired. By the twelfth, Champion and Aldaniti were leading and it was a lead that they never surrendered. At the end of the marathon four and a half miles and thirty fences, the eight hundred and fifty-six yard lung-bursting run in tested both the stamina and resolve of horse and rider. Behind them they felt the breath and heard the thunder of hoofs as Spartan Missile, ridden by fifty-four-year-old John Thorne, made ground on them and threatened to steal the headlines.

But this was to be Champion's story. Aldaniti passed the winning post four lengths ahead and another emotionally charged chapter had been written in Grand National history.

A year later Aldaniti again jumped Aintree's first fence like a novice and this time the pair parted company. But no matter. Aldaniti died at the ripe old age of twenty-seven and Bob Champion went on to raise millions of pounds for charity.

One of the upsides of being a professional jump jockey is the tight-knit camaraderie that they enjoy, drawn together by the danger and the exhilaration of the racing. Few have been more fortunate than the Irish jockey Pat Taafe, who rode a horse described by John Randall and Tony Morris in *A Century of Champions* as "a freak, an unrepeatedly lucky shake of the genetic cocktail, the nearest thing the sport has seen to the perfect machine".

Below: *The 'genetic freak' that was Arkle (on the right) on his way to winning the Cheltenham Gold Cup in 1965. Down the years there may have been better steeplechasers, but none comes to mind.*

The genetic 'freak' was an Irish bay gelding called Arkle. Trained by Tom Dreaper, another racing man with steeplechasing blood coursing through his veins, Arkle was perhaps the first chaser to become admired outside normal racing circles. He is regarded as the greatest of all time and for three winters in particular, he was several classes better than his competition – indeed a class apart from those who had come before and, in the view of most, those that have followed. Writer Ivor Herbert stated in 1966, "In Arkle's case it is the combination of speed, stamina, and jumping ability in a degree so far unequalled, which has produced the champion steeplechaser of all time."

Though his career was cut short by injury he still won three Cheltenham Gold Cups, and a host of other top prizes. In the 1964 Gold Cup he avenged a previous defeat by beating his only real adversary, Mill House, by five lengths. Such was the superiority of these two horses that only two others were entered. Indeed, the racing authorities in Ireland took the unprecedented step in the Irish Grand National of devising two weight systems – one to be used when Arkle was running and one when he wasn't. Arkle won that 1964 race by a length despite carrying two and a half stone more than his rivals.

The following year's Gold Cup saw Arkle dominate Mill House by twenty lengths, and in 1966 he won by thirty lengths despite ploughing through an early fence. He went through the 1965–6 season unbeaten in five races and at the absolute peak of his powers.

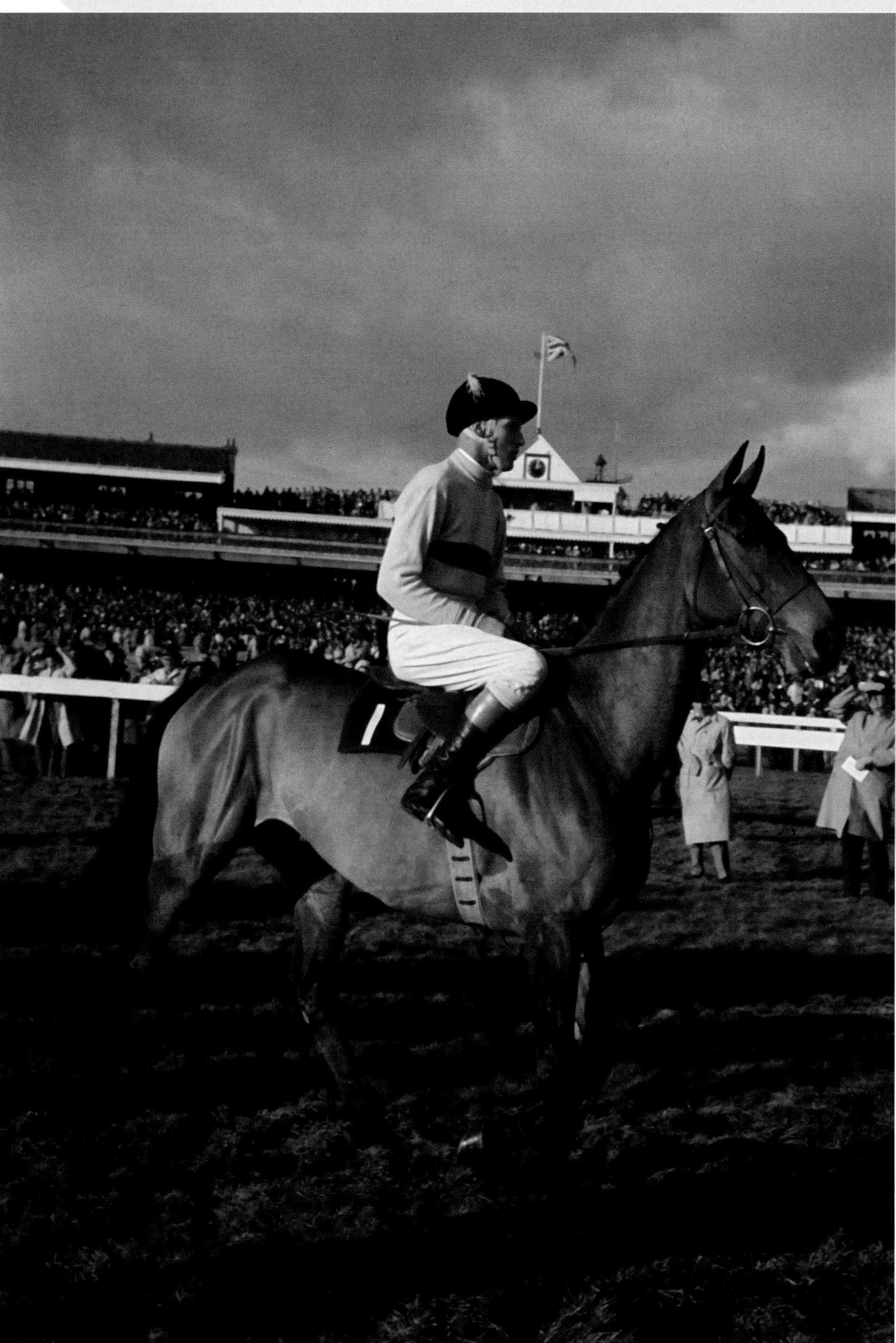

Right: *Ears pricked. Arkle at Newbury racecourse for the Hennessy Gold Cup.*

However, in the depths of the 1966 winter he struck the guard rail when jumping an open ditch in the King George VI Chase and fractured a pedal bone in his off-fore hoof. Broken bone and all, he still completed the race, finishing second. He was in plaster for four months and never raced again. In retirement he suffered with severe arthritis, or possibly brucellosis, and was put down at the early age of thirteen.

Golden Miller and Arkle both have a statue in their honour at Cheltenham. Another with that distinction is Dawn Run, who was exceptional over both hurdles and jumps. He won the Champion Hurdle in 1984, but really brought the house down in 1986 when he staged a remarkable and brave rally to catch Wayward Lad and snatch the Cheltenham Gold Cup.

A decade earlier, Red Rum had been another to make the leap – no doubt spring-heeled and clearing the obstacle by a distance – from racehorse to icon. His fame, though, was linked with Aintree, where his owner's maroon colours with yellow diamonds became well known after a five-year period of supremacy in the Grand National.

Red Rum began as a rather ordinary flat race sprinter, but having been passed from trainer to trainer he clicked with ex-Liverpool car dealer Ginger McCain who exercised him on the local beach and in the sea, partly because the horse suffered from an incurable bone disease in his foot and found the salt water therapeutic.

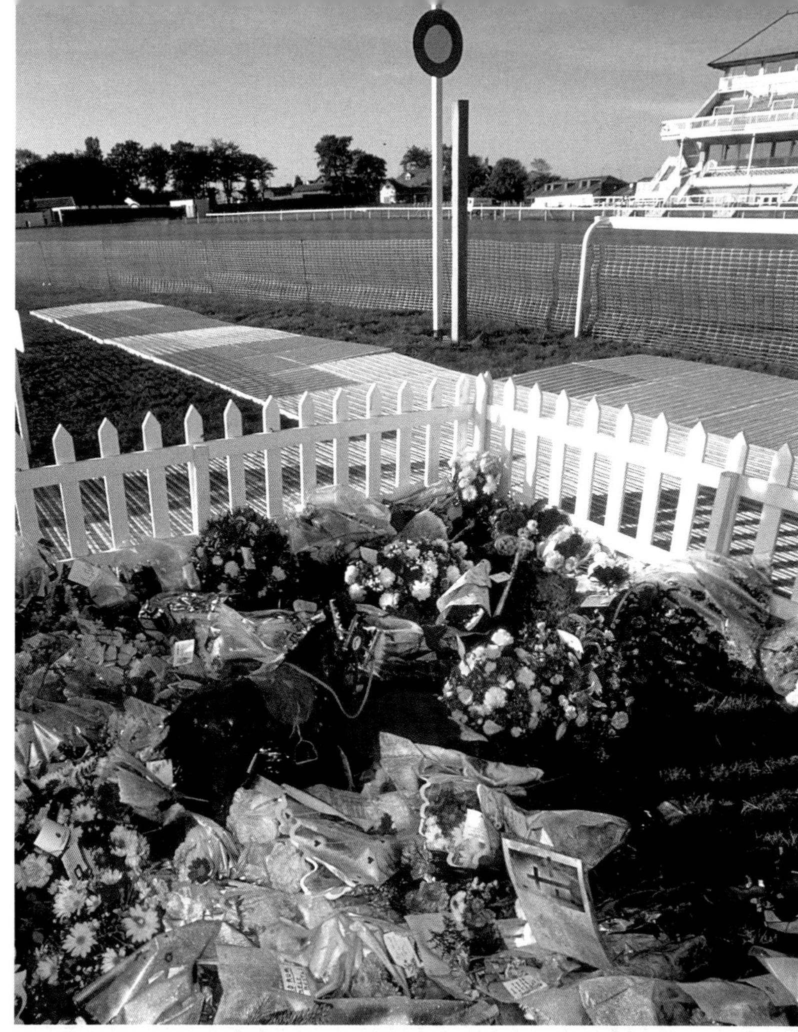

Above: *Red Rum's grave next to the winning post at Aintree. The epitaph states: "Respect this place, this hallowed ground, a legend here, his rest has found, his feet would fly, our spirits soar, he earned our love for evermore."*

One of the epics. Seven horses beat the course record at Aintree's Grand National in 1973. Here, Red Rum pips the Australian, Crisp, on the line. It was the first of three Nationals in five years for 'Rummy'.

Certainly Red Rum grew to revel on the sands at Southport and the racecourse at Aintree. He became the most successful horse in Grand National history, and for five years he demonstrated outstanding consistency in a race that many still regard as a lottery.

At one stage in the 1973 running, the Australian chaser, Crisp, had established a thirty-length lead. However, as his energy drained away he lost momentum, and two strides before the winning post Red Rum inched ahead, one of seven horses to beat the course record.

In 1974 Red Rum won again, but in 1975 – on heavy ground that did not suit him – and 1976 he finished a closely fought second behind L'Escargot and Rag Trade respectively. Then, in 1977, at twelve years of age, he conducted a master class for forty-one other runners as he left them trailing by twenty-five lengths to secure an unprecedented hat-trick. Regrettably, in 1978 a minor ailment forced his withdrawal, but by then horse and race were synonymous and he had become a celebrity, opening supermarkets and leading the pre-race parade each year.

***Right:** 1972, Cheltenham – Anne, Duchess of Westminster, unveils a bronze statue of Arkle created by local artist Doris Linder.*

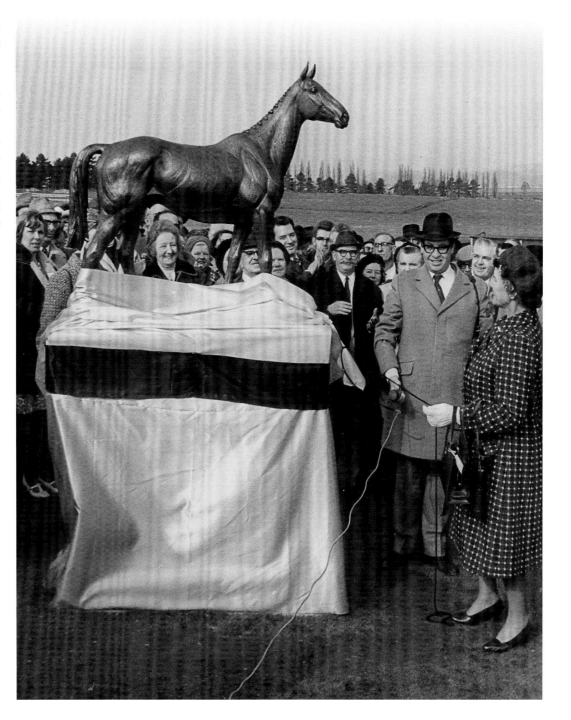

HISTORY IN THE MAKING

Epsom, 1981

The Champion-Aldaniti Grand National fairytale plastered horse racing across the back pages. A couple of months later the bay colt, Shergar, repeated the trick by winning the Epsom Derby by a record ten lengths, the biggest winning margin in the race's two hundred and twenty-six years.

Bred by his owner, Prince Karim Aga Khan IV, in County Kildare, close to the stud from which he was kidnapped, Shergar began training with Sir Michael Stoute at Newmarket. His first race in 1981 was the Guardian Classic Trial at Sandown Park, which he won by ten lengths.

After winning the Chester Vase by twelve lengths, Shergar started as odds-on favourite at Epsom, ridden by nineteen-year-old rookie Walter Swinburn.

Swinburn recalled that early in the race Shergar "found his own pace and lobbed along as the leaders went off at a million miles an hour, with me just putting my hands down on his withers and letting him travel at his own speed".

Jockey John Matthias, a distant runner-up on Glint of Gold, was only half-joking when he said, "I told myself I'd achieved my life's ambition. Only then did I discover there was another horse on the horizon."

And there they were, in the distance, the green and red of Swinburn's silks aboard the chestnut.

The phrase "Eclipse first, the rest nowhere" had found itself a modern context. Shergar had not so much outclassed the opposition as annihilated them.

Right: *Shergar, Walter Swinburn and owner, H.H. Aga Khan IV, ease through the top-hatted crowd on Derby Day on their way to the winner's enclosure.*

Right: *Swinburn drops down the gears at Epsom, yet Shergar still won by a record ten lengths.*

Swinburn later said, "When you were galloping, he was the sort you didn't realize how fast you were going because he had this really short, daisy-cutting action. He never wasted any time in the air and stayed really low. When he pulled me up to the front I remember thinking 'whooah!', but he was gone, he was on his way."

Shergar's next race was the Irish Derby Stakes which he won by four lengths at a canter. His six wins had won four hundred and thirty-six thousand pounds in prize money, before he went to stud in Ireland.

Two years later he was kidnapped one foggy evening by masked gunmen near the Ballymany Stud in Ireland. His body was never discovered and he is presumed to have been killed by his captors. The fact that his remains were never found encouraged an endless stream of conspiracy theories, and sadly Shergar's immortality owes as much to what happened after his career as it does to the demolition Derby at Epsom when racing experts were left open-mouthed in admiration.

Above: *Shergar, a truly great race horse. How unfortunate that he will also be remembered for the kidnapping and disappearance that followed his career on the racetrack.*

Ivor Herbert wrote, "Red Rum became the nation's hero by virtue of his history and character and his courageous determination to survive against the odds." However, perhaps the most fitting epitaph is the one above his burial place at the Aintree's winning post, which states, "Respect this place, this hallowed ground, a legend here, his rest has found, his feet would fly, our spirits soar, he earned our love for evermore."

Since Red Rum, the grey, Desert Orchid, has come closest to emulating this degree of accomplishment and affection. He won thirty-four of seventy-two races over a nine-year racing career. But 'Dessie' was not about statistics. It was his front-running flamboyance, love of a camera and sheer *joie de vivre* that the racing public found attractive. Having switched from hurdling to chasing, he gave jockey Richard Dunwoody many an exhilarating ride.

Left: *Desert Orchid soars, salmon-like, at Sandown racecourse. 'Dessie' had a certain devil-may-care* joie de vivre, *in his racing.*

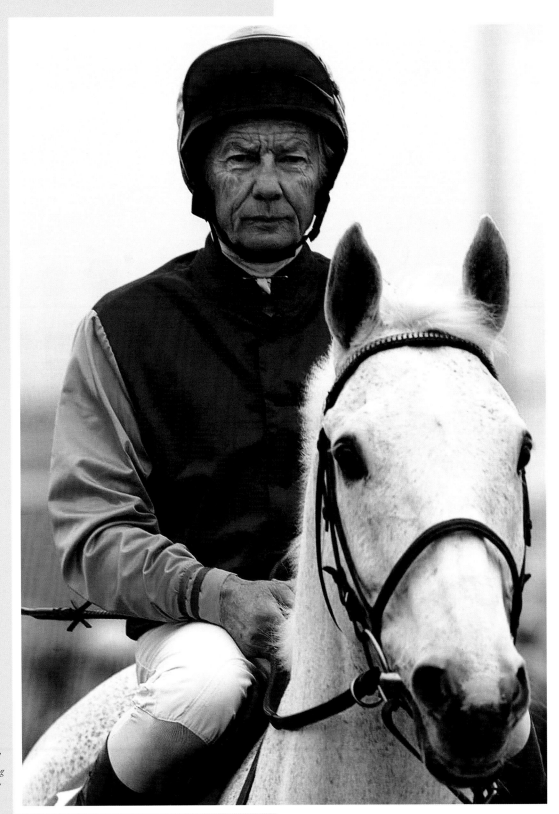

Right: *An unlikely couple. Steeplechaser Desert Orchid and the legendary flat racing jockey, Lester Piggott, in the parade ring at Wincanton.*

Chapter 9: Crowning glories

The thoroughbred racehorse is deceptively fragile. For a trainer to hone physique and sharpen fitness to enable one to contest a classic, can be as much art as science and fraught with difficulties and frustrations. There is so much that can go wrong. Tendons can tear, viruses can debilitate and temperaments and legs can be brittle – and, even if the treasured thoroughbred actually makes it to the racetrack, there is no guarantee of success. They are racing against the crème de la crème and each race only yields one winner.

So, for a trainer or owner to end in the winner's enclosure after a classic, is a notable achievement. This is only feasible through the astute preparation of a talented horse and a healthy portion of good fortune. Of course, opportunities to shine on a classic day – at least in Britain and America – are the privilege of three-year-olds only. One slip and the chance will pass forever.

To actually reach these Olympian heights and win more than one classic in a season fanfares a thoroughbred of rare quality – and to win what is known as the Triple Crown in England or America immediately places the horse in exclusive company.

Below: *Conclusive proof that you do not have to win a Triple Crown to be judged a great racehorse. Mill Reef followed up success in the 1971 Epsom Derby with this win at the Prix de l'Arc de Triomphe at Longchamp.*

Of course many have won an alternative sequence of big races. In 1971 the great Mill Reef, for example, came second in the Two Thousand Guineas, then won the Epsom Derby and the Prix de l'Arc de Triomphe. Equally there are horses that have won either the Grand National or the Melbourne Cup in successive years. And there are other 'triple crowns', in Ireland, France and Canada to name but three. However, there is something iconic and long-lasting about achieving the Triple Crown either side of the Atlantic.

The American triple consists of the Kentucky Derby, the Preakness Stakes and the Belmont Stakes, contested by three-year-olds over differing distances with little time for recuperation between races. It challenges a thoroughbred's versatility and stamina, as Dan Farley wrote in 1998: "There is no more demanding series of events in any sport than the Triple Crown, as these young horses are asked to contest three races over a five-week period."

Sir Barton was the first to achieve it in 1919, but it was in 1930 – when Gallant Fox became the second horse to win all three races – that the term Triple Crown was coined by sportswriter Charles Hatton.

Left: *June, 1971, Epsom Derby. Mill Reef ridden by Geoff Lewis is on the left of the picture as he passes the finishing post. A month earlier he had been second in the Two Thousand Guineas at Newmarket.*

As with the English classics it used to be achieved with regularity. In the period between 1930 and 1948, seven horses were successful:

1930 – Gallant Fox

1935 – Omaha

1937 – War Admiral

1941 – Whirlaway

1943 – Count Fleet

1946 – Assault

1948 Citation

The last-named became the first to earn more than one million U.S. dollars in prize money. Thereafter, the feats of endurance became much scarcer, and when Secretariat won the 1973 U.S. Triple Crown, he was the first to do so in twenty-five years. But then he was a horse that broke the mould – perhaps the horse of the century.

Born in Virginia, Secretariat was a large, bright-red chestnut

Above: *Play time. A charming snapshot of the great Secretariat at his leisure in stables at Louisville, Kentucky.*

Left: *Time to work. Secretariat powers to the Preakness Stakes at Pimlico in 1973. This was the middle leg of the Triple Crown in America.*

colt, with three white socks and a blaze. Like the famous Man o' War, he became known as 'Big Red', ultimately standing an athletic sixteen hands, two inches tall. "Trying to fault Secretariat's conformation was like dreaming of dry rain," penned U.S. sportswriter Charlie Hatton.

He ran in Penny Chenery's colours of blue and white chequered silks, was trained by Canadian Lucien Laurin and ridden by fellow Canadian jockey Ron Turcotte.

He finished fourth in his first race at Aqueduct racetrack when he was impeded at the start, but then won five in a row, including the Sanford Stakes, the Hopeful Stakes and the Futurity Stakes. He then finished first in the Champagne Stakes at Belmont, but was placed second for interfering. He avenged that loss in the Laurel Futurity, and completed his season with a win in the Garden State Futurity. Secretariat was named Horse of the Year at two, so hopes were high for a successful season as a three-year-old.

Below: *Jockey Ron Turcotte enjoys the moment after Secretariat wins the 1973 Kentucky Derby at Churchill Downs. One down, two to go.*

Below: *Secretariat (number fourteen) at the back of the field after the start of the Kentucky Derby in 1973. He broke late but did not stay there for long and won with ease.*

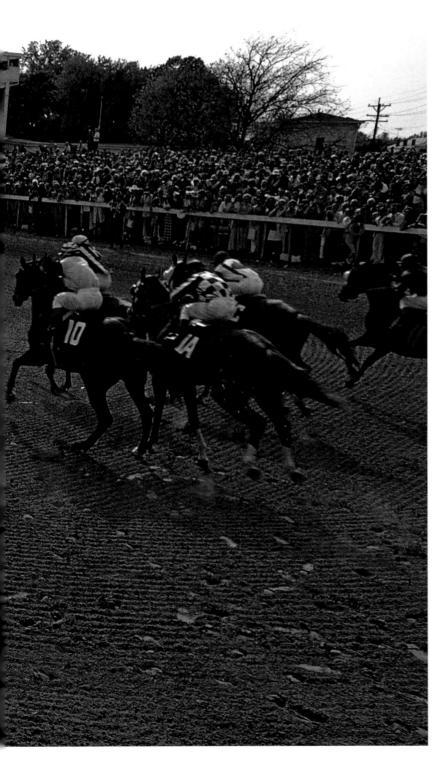

He won in the Bay Shore Stakes at Aqueduct, and the Gotham Stakes, where he equalled the track record, before finishing third in the Wood Memorial in the warm-up race for the Kentucky Derby, suffering with a boil in his mouth. Despite this defeat he began as favourite at Churchill Downs. He broke last but progressively moved through the field then overtook his arch rival Sham at the top of the stretch, pulling away to win by two and a half lengths.

Timekeepers were able to validate just what a ground-breaking performance it had been. As he created a track record, he covered each quarter-mile segment faster than the one before it. He had moved through the gears like no other horse before him. It would be twenty-eight years before any other horse ran the Derby in less than two minutes.

His masterful form continued in the Preakness Stakes when he broke late again but then made a last-to-first move on the first turn. After reaching the lead with five and a half furlongs to go he was never challenged and won by two and a half lengths from Sham.

Two out of two and he had become a national luminary as he prepared for the Belmont Stakes, appearing on the covers of three notable American magazines, *Time, Newsweek* and *Sports Illustrated*. As Jack Whittaker said at the opening of the CBS television broadcast from Belmont, "There may be some people who do not know who or what Secretariat is – people who have been marooned on Pacific Islands or lost in Amazonian jungles."

Above: *A class apart and all alone. The Belmont Stakes, in New York, which Secretariat won by thirty-one lengths. Moments of such dominance are rare in sport; this one deserves a treasured place in the legends.*

Only four horses joined him for the race, including Sham. The weather was sizzling but Secretariat was ice-cool in the paddock, and in front of sixty-seven thousand spectators he was, for once, quickly into his stride. Along with Sham, they soon opened ten lengths on the rest of the field. After the six furlong mark, Sham began to tire, ultimately finishing last, but Secretariat astonished spectators by maintaining the lung-bursting pace, creating a cavernous margin on the field. He covered the first mile in just over one minute, thirty-four seconds, by which time he led by seven lengths. By the start of the home straight he was twenty lengths ahead and when he won by a record breaking thirty-one lengths the clock showed that he had just run the fastest one and a half miles on dirt in history: two minutes, twenty-four seconds.

That was a hard act to follow, but within five years Seattle Slew and Affirmed had also secured a Triple Crown success. 'The Slew' cost just seventeen thousand U.S. dollars when he was purchased as a yearling in Kentucky, but his value soared after he followed Secretariat in becoming the champion two-year-old and then storming to wins of one and three-quarter lengths, one and a half lengths and four lengths at Churchill Downs, Pimlico and Belmont respectively. In February 1978 a half share in him was sold for six million dollars.

Above: *Seattle Slew and jockey Jean Cruguet pull ahead of the pack to win the Kentucky Derby at Churchill Downs in 1977.*

Left: *1978. Steve Cauthen ushers Affirmed (number six) to the Preakness Stakes at Pimlico. Thirty-five years on, Affirmed remains the most recent winner of the U.S. Triple Crown. Riches await those who can break the drought.*

Later that year Affirmed became the most recent winner of the Triple Crown. He was ridden by Steve Cauthen who said, "He was probably the most intelligent horse I was ever around. He had a lot of common sense, he loved to run and battle, and he was an easy horse to ride. I just appreciated his company." Writer Patrick Robinson added his own eulogy: "If there has been a more superlative example of stern, unrelenting courage in a thoroughbred horse, no one has yet made it public."

In the thirty-five years since, no horse has emulated the feats of Secretariat, Seattle Slew and Affirmed – but rest assured that a place in the legends awaits the one that does.

In England, there are two versions of the Triple Crown, one for colts and one for fillies. The colts' version features the Two Thousand Guineas, the Epsom Derby (both of which tend to be contested solely by colts) and the St Leger. The fillies' equivalent is the One Thousand Guineas, the Oaks and the St Leger.

The colts' Triple Crown was first achieved in 1853 by West Australian, and in the nineteenth century it was fairly common, with seven other thoroughbreds putting their names in lights. They were:

1865 – Gladiateur

1866 – Lord Lyon

1886 – Ormonde

1891 – Common

1893 – Isinglass

1897 – Galtee More

1899 – Flying Fox

In the twentieth century this trend continued, with another five Triple Crown winners in the first nineteen seasons:

1900 – Diamond Jubilee

1903 – Rock Sand

1915 – Pommern

1917 – Gay Crusader

1918 – Gainsborough

But after the First World War it became far less common as the competition grew stronger. It was another seventeen years before Bahram won in 1935, and another thirty-five until Nijinsky in 1970. And in the forty-three years since? Nothing. The feat is almost obsolete, and until recently only Nashwan in 1989 had even won the first two legs. This was matched by Sea the Stars in 2009 and Camelot in 2012.

Left: *In 1853 West Australian became the first horse to win the English Triple Crown (colts) of Two Thousand Guineas, Epsom Derby and St Leger.*

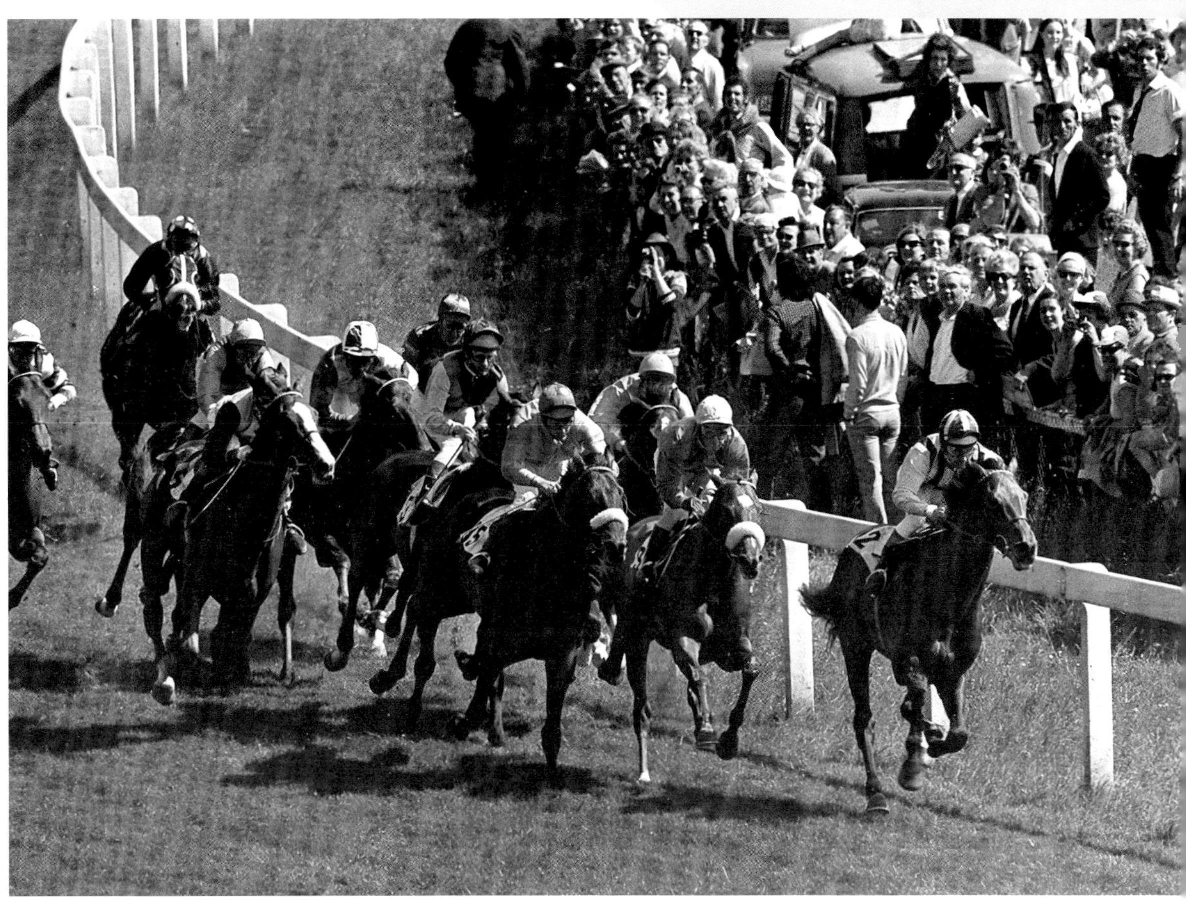

Above: *June, 1970. The pack makes the turn around Tattenham Corner into the home straight at Epsom. Poised to strike, the victor to be is Nijinsky (number three in fifth place) ridden by Lester Piggott.*

***Below:** The third and final jewel in the Triple Crown. Nijinksy wins the St Leger at Doncaster. Before the race he suffered with ringworm, but on raceday his quality shone through.*

So Nijinsky's achievement assures him of a place in the pantheon of the sport. The son of Northern Dancer, the great Canadian colt who had stormed to the Kentucky Derby, Nijinsky was bought as a yearling in 1968 in Canada for eighty-four thousand dollars by Charles Engelhard who sent him to the doyen of trainers, Vincent O'Brien in Ireland. This was just as well. Nijinsky took some handling. He was a complicated, high maintenance character; excitable, impatient, highly strung, a fussy eater and an erratic trainer. But the effort was worth it because on a racetrack he travelled as though he had dynamite in his hoofs and wings on his back. In his two-year-old campaign he won five races out of five, four in Ireland followed by the Dewhurst Stakes in Newmarket.

As a three-year-old he extended the unbeaten record with a warm-up win at the Curragh before he returned to H.Q. for his first tilt at a classic, Newmarket's Two Thousand Guineas. Doubts remained over his temperament and sure enough he sweated up profusely in the pre-race parade, but his class shone through when the race began and he won easily from Yellow God.

Some misgivings still existed when he arrived in front of the vast crowds on Epsom Downs. Aside from that dubious disposition, some felt that the distance and going might not suit. They could not have been more wrong. Jockey Lester Piggott kept him calm during the preliminaries, and a couple of reminders during the race encouraged him to pick up the pace past French challenger, Gyr, to secure classic number two.

Nijinsky retained his form through the summer, winning the Irish Derby, and the King George VI and Queen Elizabeth Stakes at Royal Ascot. But come autumn and the third and final leg at Doncaster he suffered an attack of ringworm. He temporarily lost hair down one flank and could not have been at his peak on raceday. Yet he won the St Leger to secure what remains the most recent clean sweep of the classics. He went to stud in Kentucky at the end of the season with a glittering record to his name.

__Above:__ A free flowing Oh So Sharp at the St Leger.

The quest for the fillies' Triple Crown in England has followed a similar pattern in that it appears to have become more and more difficult to achieve. There were three winners in seven years between 1868 and 1874, including Formosa, who was also entered for, and won, the colts-dominated Two Thousand Guineas. Another who took on the colts and won was Sceptre who claimed all of the English classics in 1902 with the exception of the Derby where she finished fourth. But since 1955 there has just been the one Triple Crown winner, Oh So Sharp.

The full list is:

1868 – Formosa

1871 – Hannah

1874 – Apology

1892 – La Fleche

1902 – Sceptre

1904 – Pretty Polly

1942 – Sun Chariot

1955 – Meld

1985 – Oh So Sharp

Owned by Sheikh Mohammed, trained by that ace teacher of fillies, Sir Henry Cecil, and ridden by top American jockey, Steve Cauthen, Oh So Sharp benefited from an ideal combination of connections. Her victory in the One Thousand Guineas was tight, by two short heads over Al Bahathri and Bella Colora, but in the Oaks the margin was six lengths and she sealed the triple at Doncaster.

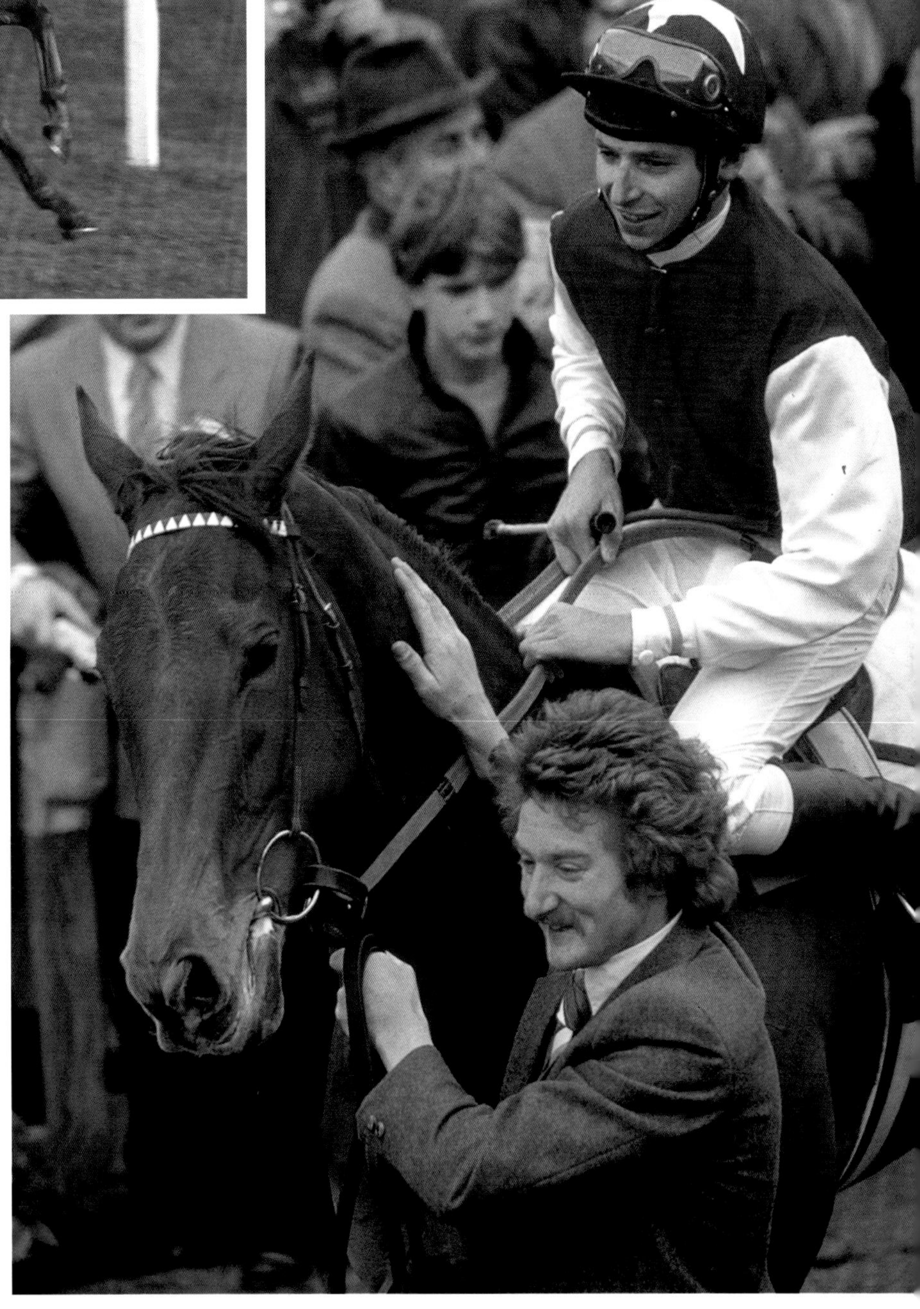

__Right:__ Oh So Sharp is led in after the One Thousand Guineas at Newmarket in 1985. Steve Cauthen on board. He went on to win the Epsom Derby and the St Leger to secure the fillies' Triple Crown.

HISTORY IN THE MAKING

Ascot, 1996

When Frankie Dettori turned up for work at Ascot racecourse on Saturday 28th September 1996 it felt much like any other day. When someone asked him how he thought he would perform during his seven rides he replied, "I could have an each-way chance in the first and I may win the third."

The extrovert Dettori was not normally inclined toward understatement but, on this occasion, the way that the day panned out proved that he had been unduly downbeat with his prognosis.

In the first race, for instance, he rode his 'each-way chance' Wall Street to a half a length win in a group three race.

Dettori was even more pessimistic about his chance in the second. He told the travelling head lad, "I'll bare my bum under the Newmarket clock tower if he wins." But the horse, Diffident, a twelve to one chance, won by a short head in a three-way finish. Two out of two. A group two secured.

Dettori was, however, right about race three. He rode the Two Thousand Guineas winner, Mark of Esteem, to a group one triumph. He was so impressed by the horse's turn of foot that he described it as the "best performance of any miler I've ridden". Three out of three.

The easiest win of the day was on Decorated Hero, three and a half lengths the distance. Dettori raised four fingers in triumph as he entered the winner's enclosure. He was growing aware of the possibilities, the increasing excitement of racegoers and the nervousness of the bookmakers who were now considering the possibility of some significant losses.

In the fifth race, Fatefully was a red-hot favourite but only won by a whisker and also survived a steward's enquiry. In the sixth, Lochangel secured a three-quarters of a length victory. Dettori had equalled the record and was fully 'in the zone', riding at the top of his ability. He later recalled, "Horses have the ability to catch your mood and the horses caught my mood that day. I wasn't even on the ground – I was flying and they were running just that little bit faster."

Right: *Seventh heaven. The famous Dettori flying dismount celebrates one of racing's more awe-inspiring afternoons.*

Before the seventh and last race, Dettori and his mount, Fujiyama Crest, got a standing ovation on the way to the start, though not from the bookmakers, some of whom were facing financial ruin.

He won! By a neck. The first jockey to win every race on a seven-race card. An unprecedented twenty-five thousand to one accumulator that put several bookmakers out of business.

Later, Dettori considered how the feat compared with his Derby win in 2007 with Authorized: "Well, the Derby was just one race; Ascot was seven in one day. In three hundred years of horse racing I'm the first one to have ever done it (seven winners in a day) and I'm probably the first living person to have a statue (Dettori's statue, commemorating the achievement, stands at Ascot). Normally you only have a statue when you're dead!"

Below: *Dettori celebrates after victory on Fujiyama Crest in the seventh and final race.*

Below: *Dettori again. This time he soaks up the adulation after a win on the talented Mark of Esteem in the Queen Elizabeth II Stakes at Ascot.*

The New Classics

Chapter 10: New Horizons

In the sixty years after the Prix de l'Arc de Triomphe was first run at Longchamp in 1920 the horse racing calendar remained relatively static. In Europe, America and Australia there was an established infrastructure of racecourses and race meetings that had helped the sport to find itself a cosy niche in the entertainment industry.

However, in the same way that horses such as Eclipse signalled a quantum leap in the evolution of thoroughbreds, the last two decades of the twentieth century saw new blue riband events become inked in on the racing calendar. With worldwide travel easier and cheaper than before, the call went out to owners and trainers around the world: come to Japan, come to Hong Kong, above all come to Dubai, and compete for prestige and life-changing amounts of prize money.

These new events were strategically positioned in the year to make it as easy as possible for the crème de la crème to attend and, sure enough, they came, like moths to the flame from the traditional strongholds.

In Japan, for instance, horse racing had long been popular, with crowds often exceeding one hundred thousand, and there was a strong gambling culture. However, the Japan Cup, first run in 1981 in Tokyo, emphasized the country as a key player in the sport. Annually contested on the last Sunday in November by three-year-olds and upwards, it immediately proved alluring. Grundy and Dancing Brave are two examples from Europe who made the trip, as did five consecutive winners of the Epsom Derby in the 1990s, including Lammtarra. Over thirty years on, the race has established itself as a genuinely international contest with winners from Japan, North America, Britain, Australia, New Zealand, Ireland, France, Germany and Italy. Partially as a result, Japan has made big strides in the world of bloodstock with many top racehorses going there to stand at stud.

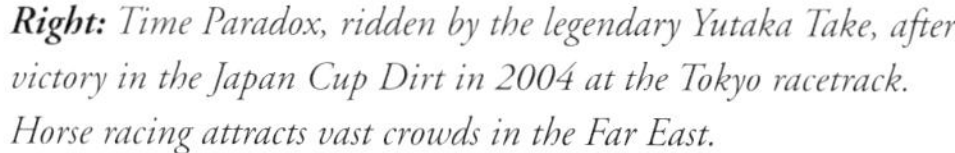

Right: *Time Paradox, ridden by the legendary Yutaka Take, after victory in the Japan Cup Dirt in 2004 at the Tokyo racetrack. Horse racing attracts vast crowds in the Far East.*

Equally, the Hong Kong Cup, first run in 1988, has raised its country's own sporting profile. The Happy Valley racetrack became established in 1978 and also hosted vast crowds and extensive gambling. However, the Hong Kong Jockey Club were astute enough to build upon this foundation by implementing the Hong Kong Cup, a race for three-year-olds and upwards contested in December at the Sha Tin racecourse.

The first race was restricted to horses trained in Hong Kong, Malaysia and Singapore. But, subsequently, invitations have been extended to Australia and New Zealand (since 1989), Europe (1990), the United States of America (1991) and Canada and Japan (1992). The race currently offers a purse close to three million U.S. dollars.

It was also in the 1980s that John R. Gaines, a prominent breeder and owner of the Gainesway Farm in Lexington, Kentucky, saw to it that America also contributed an exciting addition to the international racing calendar.

He wanted to create an equine equivalent to the stature and profile of a Super Bowl or World Series. To do that he needed the best thoroughbreds from East and West on American soil – and he hoped to create an international focal point at the end of the season. His vision was for one glorious day of races, each different in nature. He saw opportunities for the best colts and fillies, of all ages, to compete over a variety of distances. To lure them he needed serious prize money, so he determined that each of the races would offer a pot of at least one million dollars.

Left: *Globe-trotting Italian Frankie Dettori rides Ramonti to victory in the 2007 Hong Kong Cup at the Sha Tin racecourse.*

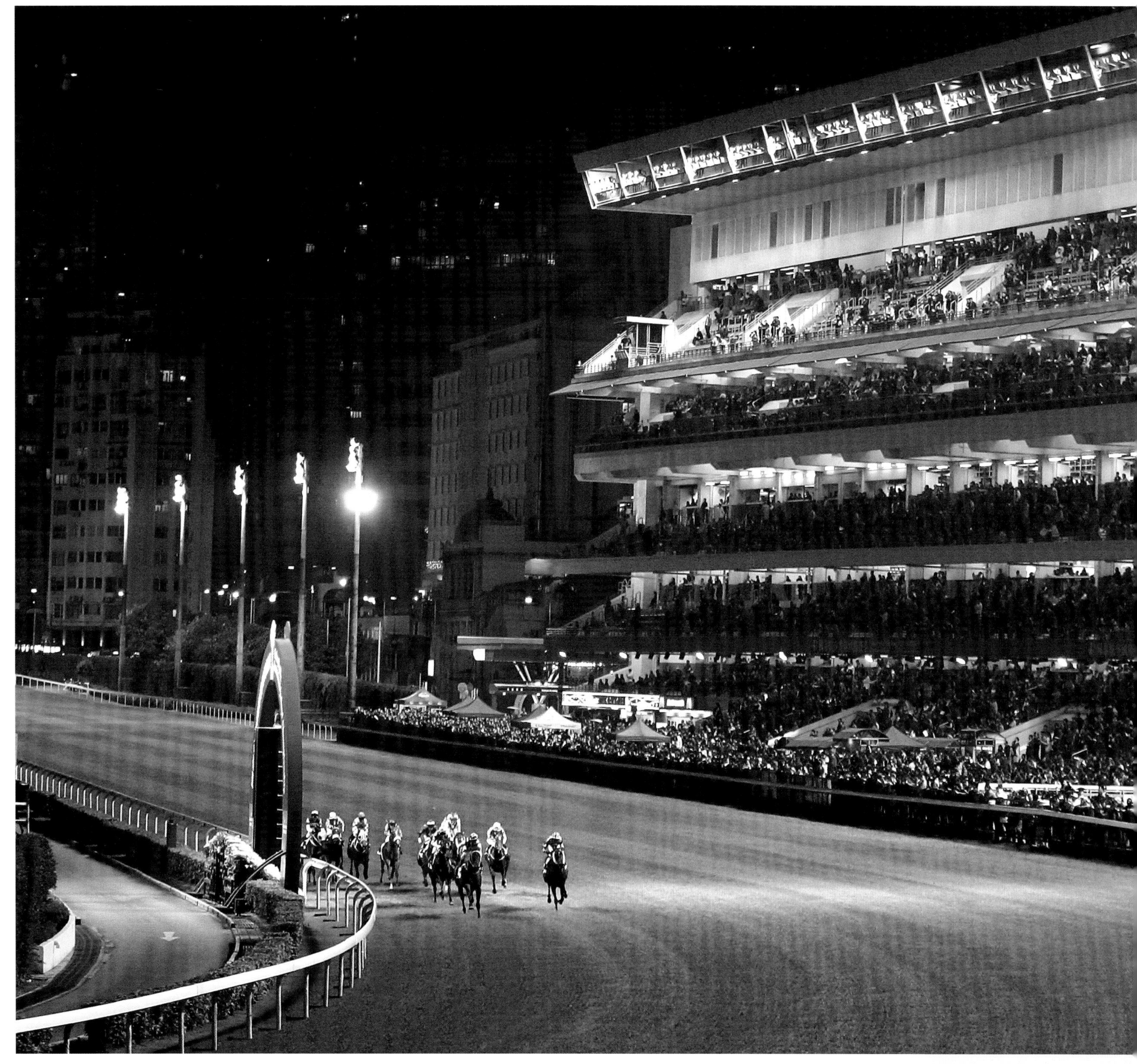

Of course, conceiving the vision was easy compared with making it happen. Some observers were pessimistic. Before it had even been organized, the American magazine *Blood-Horse* remarked, "The Breeders' Cup is in trouble. Its detractors are many, for myriad reasons, and as of writing it seems about to be buried under layer upon layer of criticism." Yet, on a positive note, it added, "the idea is too good to die".

Gaines needed support and the breeding industry eventually supplied it, generating the necessary prize money by annual nomination payments for stallions and one-time nomination fees for those stallions' offspring.

Eight eager racetracks bid for the first running and it was Hollywood Park in California that got the vote. Sixty-two thousand turned out on 10th November 1984 for the first meeting, with millions more watching on television. It has now continued for nearly thirty years at a variety of locations across the country, notably Kentucky's Churchill Downs, Hollywood Park and Santa Anita in California, Belmont Park in New York and Florida's Gulfstream Park. The event has become an important and popular part of the American sporting landscape. Whether it has become bigger than the Kentucky Derby is a moot point, but there is no doubt that the inspiration of John Gaines has been richly rewarded.

Left: *Evening racing at the Happy Valley racecourse in Hong Kong possesses a dramatic feel and a true sense of occasion. Horse racing has evolved greatly since the first plots of suitable territory were discovered amidst England's green and pleasant land.*

So by the end of the twentieth century there were horses with full passports. Horses like Pilsudski, trained by Sir Michael Stoute. In four seasons he raced with great distinction in Britain, Ireland, France, Germany, Canada and Japan. Victory at the 1996 Breeders' Cup Turf in Toronto, victory in the 1997 Japan Cup, two second places in the Prix de l'Arc de Triomphe; this was a frequent traveller par excellence.

However, despite gleaming new events in Japan, Hong Kong and America, perhaps the single most influential development at the end of the twentieth century was the fervour for horse racing shown by the affluent ruling family of Dubai.

Below: *Horses break from the gate at the start of the Breeders' Cup Classic at Santa Anita in California. It is another popular venue for the Breeders' Cup. The winner of this 2008 running was Raven's Pass, third from left, ridden by Frankie Dettori.*

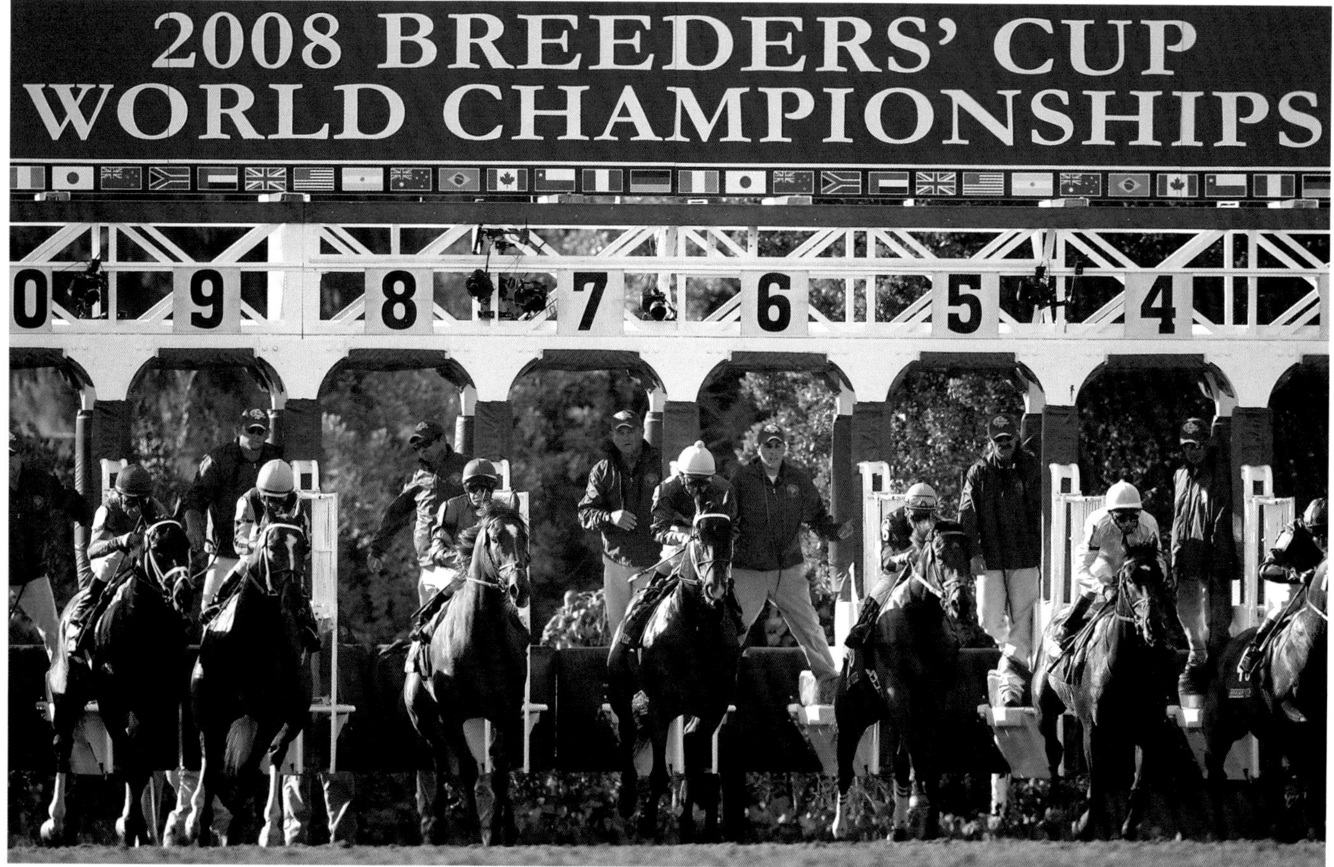

Left: *The Hollywood Park racetrack in California. A regular venue for the Breeders' Cup which moves from location to location to share the drama and spectacle around America.*

Right: *Saint Liam ridden by Jerry Bailey wins the 2005 Breeders' Cup Classic on the dirt track at Belmont Park in New York.*

Below: *Another frequent Breeders' Cup venue: Gulfstream Park in Hallandale Beach in Florida. Bathed in early morning sunshine, a gentle workout for the Lemon Drop Kidd in 1999.*

Sheikh Rashid bin Saeed Al-Maktoum and his sons – Sheikh Maktoum, Sheikh Hamdan, Sheikh Mohammed and Sheikh Ahmed – changed the face of racing, particularly in Europe, as they became enthusiastic and driven owners.

Sheikh Maktoum was the oldest of the brothers and was the first to claim an English classic with Touching Wood in the 1982 St Leger.

Sheikh Hamdan's colours of royal blue, white epaulets, striped cap are a familiar sight around the world. He won the Melbourne Cup in 1986 with Al Taraq and in 1994 with Jeune, and has won the Derby and Two Thousand Guineas twice. He was leading owner in Britain in 1990, 1994, 1995, 2002 and 2005.

Sheikh Ahmed is the youngest of the four brothers, landing his first classic in the One Thousand Guineas in 2001 with Ameerat.

Perhaps the most influential and ambitious has been Sheikh Mohammed. He won the English Triple Crown in 1985 with Oh So Sharp, and for more than thirty years has owned a powerful string of thoroughbreds. He was always intent on winning races of the highest standard, but he learned that bloodstock ownership brought low-profile satisfaction.

"If a horse is owned by the Queen or George Smith or me, it does not matter, it is the trainer's name that is always going to be attached to the horse," he once said, "the poor owner is not going to be mentioned at all in the whole story. He is only there to pay the bills and to be told where the horse will run. I tried and tried to alter this and, really, I just gave up."

Above: *A first classic for Sheikh Ahmed. Ameerat (number one) lands the One Thousand Guineas at Newmarket in 2001. The influence of the Maktoum brothers transformed the sport.*

Left: *Pilsudski wins the Breeders' Cup Turf Race on Canadian soil at the Woodbine racetrack in Toronto. Pilsudksi raced with great distinction all over the world, his exploits underlining that the nature of horse racing had changed as the twenty-first century approached. The racing world had become smaller as its popularity increased.*

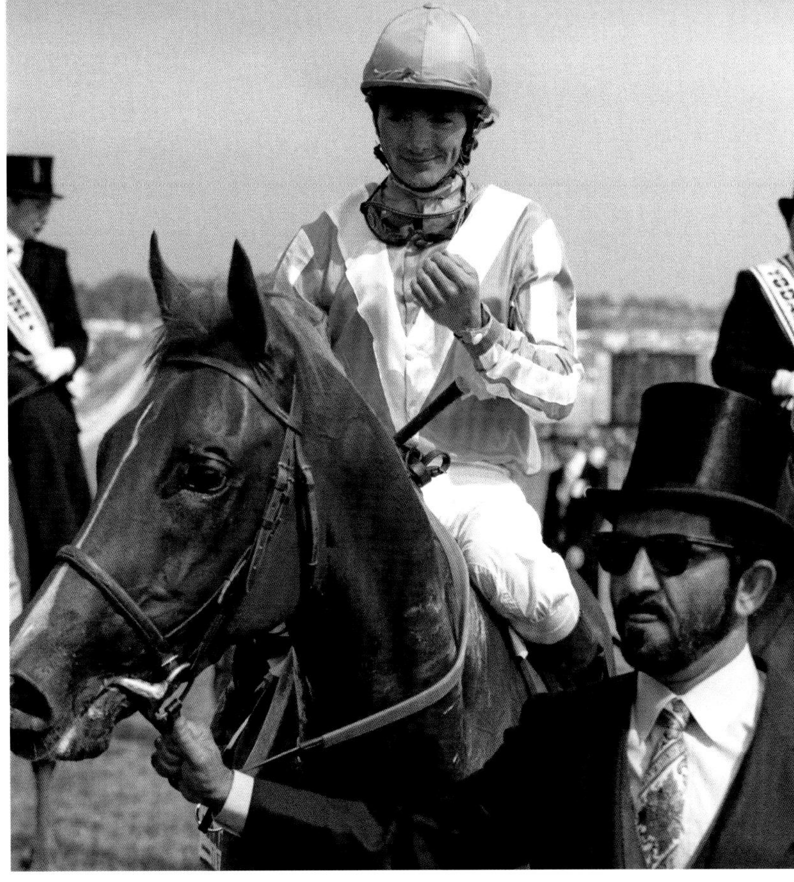

Perhaps it was this, along with a desire to place the tiny but prosperous Emirates state of Dubai on the racing map, that encouraged him to spread his influence into not only ownership but also breeding and training.

In 1981 Sheikh Mohammed purchased the Gainsborough Stud in Berkshire, England, and followed up by purchasing the Ballysheehan Stud in Ireland and the Gainsborough Farms in Kentucky, America.

And then he became the leading partner in the Godolphin training operation, which took its name from one of the founding stallions, the Godolphin Arabian. It established opulent, well-equipped stables in both Dubai and Moulton Paddocks in Newmarket, England, with the idea that the fortunate thoroughbreds wintered with the sun on their backs before travelling back to England each spring.

The first horses to run as Godolphin ran in 1994, and Balanchine was just beaten in the One Thousand Guineas at their very first attempt at securing a classic. But they did not have to wait long. The horse won the Oaks and the Irish Derby that year.

In 1995 Saaed bin Suroor became a new trainer for Godolphin and many of the Maktoum-owned horses were funnelled into his care, with great success. That year Lammtarra won the Epsom Derby and the Prix de l'Arc de Triomphe, Monshell the Oaks, and Classic Cliché the St Leger. In 1996 Mark of Esteem won the Two Thousand Guineas. And so it went on. Godolphin had become a dominant force and still is, twenty years on. Wherever big races are contested it is almost certain that their racing silks will be visible in the shake-up down the stretch. Nor is that interest showing signs of diminishing. In 2008 Sheikh Mohammed bought the Woodlands Stud, the largest in Australia, for four hundred and twenty million U.S. dollars, and 2012 saw over 200 winners in Godolphin colours, earning the stable close to twenty-six million U.S. dollars.

Top: *1995. Lammtarra wins the Epsom Derby and is led in by Saeed Al-Maktoum. The jockey is Walter Swinburn.*

Left: *Another classic victory for the boys in blue. Godolphin's Classic Cliché wins the St Leger at Doncaster in 1995.*

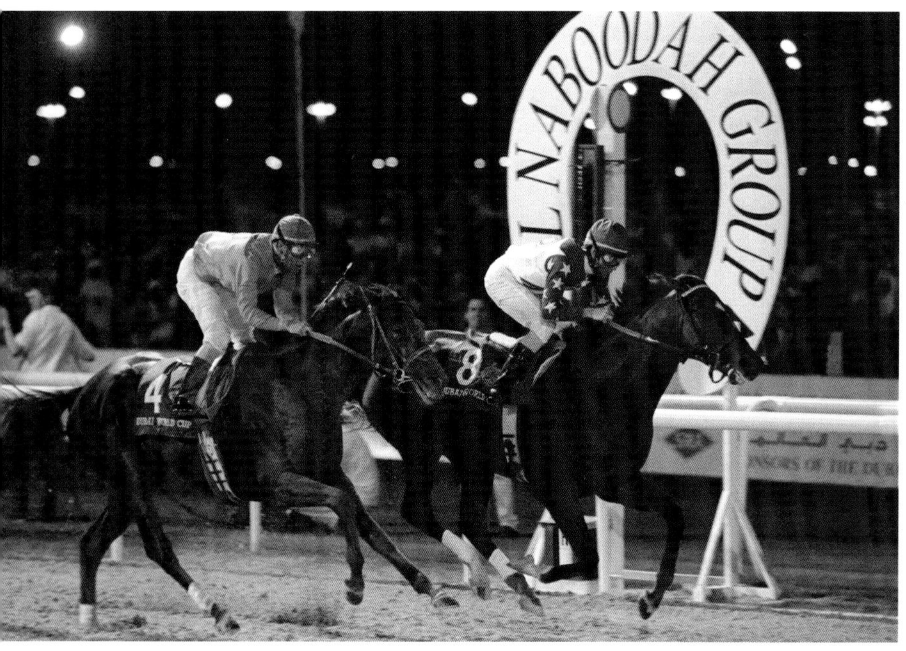

However, he points out that this is not all about the acquisition of power. "People tend to get the wrong idea about the attitude to racing," he said in 1998. "We do not want to throw our weight around. We enjoy our horses. We do not bet. We run our horses fairly and we thoroughly enjoy racing."

Nevertheless, that desire to promote Dubai had already led him to mastermind the creation of the Dubai World Cup, the world's richest series of horse races, first held at Nad al Shaba, the state's principal racecourse, which was extensively redeveloped and renamed Meydan Racecourse in 2010.

Nad al Shaba's first meeting took place in 1992 and on the 27th March 1996 it hosted the first running of the Dubai World Cup, contested over one and a quarter miles for four-year-olds and upwards. Again the prize was so valuable that it attracted the world's top middle-distance horses.

Sure enough, among the horses entered in the inaugural race were a thirteen-time winner from Australia, a seven-race winner from Great Britain, the 'dirt horse' champion from Japan, and Cigar, North America's Horse of the Year for 1995. And it was Cigar, a specialist on dirt, who won his fourteenth successive win, narrowly beating Soul of the Matter. Four years later, the race's status was sealed when Frankie Dettori accompanied Dubai Millennium to a six-length cruise to victory.

Thereafter the Dubai World Cup was there to stay, and even though there is no gambling at the racecourse large crowds make the journey to Dubai each November, underlining that the state and the Maktoums are also there to stay in racing's new world order.

Not only do visitors enjoy the contest. To add to the sense of occasion Dubai precedes the race with a week of festivities including huge parties in the desert that have acted as a joyous advertisement for the state and the United Arab Emirates.

However, Godolphin does not have it all its own way and has a healthy, though intensely competitive, rivalry with Coolmore. The Coolmore team was established by the partnership of legendary trainer, Vincent O'Brien, owner-breeder Robert Sangster and John Magnier when they took over a three hundred and fifty acre property in Ireland in 1975. Nearly forty years on, their operation has mushroomed and it is now a multinational, multimillion-pound, booming business. Coolmore's studs can also be found in the United States and Australia, and they have a specifically adapted Boeing 747 to transport their suitably pampered bloodstock around the planet.

Magnier heads Coolmore's current management team, with Michael Tabor and Aidan O'Brien as close associates. O'Brien trains most of the horses from the studs and has been immensely successful in winning big races.

And so, particularly in Europe, the nature of racing ownership as it entered the final throes of the twentieth century had changed. The rise of Godolphin and Coolmore, plus other operations in their image, meant that the elite horses tended to be owned by the privileged few who were able to build up a team of superbly bred horses through their own breeding operations and by heavy investment at bloodstock auctions.

Above left: *The first Dubai World Cup in 1996. Jerry Bailey on Cigar (number eight) wins the four million dollar prize by half a length. Cigar was an outstanding performer, an expert on dirt, who gave the new event immediate stature and profile by his attendance and hard-earned victory.*

Left: *A Dubai dawn has just broken over Nad al Sheba, once home of the Dubai World Cup. Dubai is a prominent player in the modern world of racing.*

Above right: *A meeting of minds. John Magnier, John Halley and Aidan O'Brien survey an early morning workout. They possess some of the sharpest brains in racing.*

Right: *Allen Paulson, owner of Cigar, is presented with the Dubai World Cup by the King of Dubai.*

HISTORY IN THE MAKING

Flemington, 2003, 2004, 2005

One of the beauties of handicaps such as the Melbourne Cup and England's Grand National is that, because they are not restricted to certain age ranges, it is possible to race and maybe win more than once, thereby creating a storyline that can build from year to year. The public gets to identify with the heroes. Red Rum's exploits at the Grand National over five years was a great example, his reputation growing with each new feat – and Makybe Diva was the Melbourne Cup's equivalent.

Previously four colts, Archer, Peter Pan, Rain Lover and Think Big, had won the Cup twice, but 'The Diva', as she became known, surpassed them all and ended as the biggest equine prize winner in Australian history with more than fourteen million Australian dollars to her name.

In 2003, after finishing fourth in the Caulfield Cup, she began her partnership with Sydney jockey Glen Boss and won her first Melbourne Cup. Starting as second favourite, she cruised at the back of the field until the finishing straight, where Boss picked his way through the field to win by one and a half lengths. That year she also became the first mare to ever win the Sydney Cup and Melbourne Cup double in the same season. Only four other horses have accomplished the feat.

After the 2003–4 season, trainer David Hall left to train in Hong Kong, and Makybe Diva transferred to Lee Freedman, who had already won the Melbourne Cup three times before, with Tawrrific in 1989, Subzero in 1992, and Doriemus in 1995.

Calling upon this experience and a proven track record, Freedman tailored Makybe Diva's 2004 campaign to winning the Melbourne Cup for a second time. In the Caulfield Cup she was narrowly defeated by arch rival Elvstroem, but was still favourite as she ploughed through driving rain to win Melbourne Cup number two with a top quality field – including Irish St Leger winner Vinnie Rose, Caulfield Cup winners Mummify and Elvstroem, Godolphin's Mamool and the 2002 Melbourne Cup winner Media Puzzle – trailing in her wake.

When the rain-splattered jockey Glen Boss was complimented on the ride he replied with typical honesty, "Makybe Diva is the legend, I'm just the lucky bastard who is sitting on her back."

***Right:** Jockey Glen Boss waves to the crowds and celebrates after steering Makybe Diva, for the second year running, to victory in the Melbourne Cup in 2004.*

And on 1st November 2005, Makybe Diva defied the odds by creating history to win a record third Melbourne Cup. Greatly to her credit she had not been burdened by the weight of expectation and the handicapping system that penalizes previous successes and maturity. She carried over nine stone that day, though it seemed to make little difference.

Immediately after the race, trainer Lee Freedman said of the achievement: "Go find the smallest child on this course, and there will be the only example of a person who will live long enough to see that again." During the presentation of the Melbourne Cup, owner Tony Santic announced that Makybe Diva would "retire from racing as of today". She was honoured at Flemington racecourse with a bronze statue.

Just occasionally every sport needs a superstar contestant to generate new interest and widen its appeal – and Makybe Diva was an excellent conduit to help share with a wider audience what Australia already knew: that the Melbourne Cup is fair dinkum.

Below: *Makybe Diva strides out past the winning post in classic style to secure her first Melbourne Cup.*

Above: *1st November 2005. The history-making three in a row. More jubilation for Boss. Makybe Diva seems to be taking it in her impressive stride despite carrying more than nine stone.*

Chapter 11: Twenty-first Century – Global and prosperous

So after four centuries of evolution where has horse racing progressed to? What has changed and what has stayed the same? Is it moving forward or back? Is the future bright or have its halcyon days long gone?

Any meaningful analysis needs to begin with the very framework and structure of the sport and the way that the rules and regulations that became formalized by the various Jockey Clubs have changed and evolved. Naturally, the nature and rate of the changes have differed around the world, but many have become accepted as good practice.

Above: *They're off! The stalls open to herald another race at Chantilly racecourse in France in 2006. Stalls are a comparatively modern innovation; in the early days, races were started by the cry of "Go!"*

Take the way that races are set in motion. Thankfully this has progressed from the amateurish shout of "Go" that began races in the days of Flying Childers and Eclipse. It moved to the waving of a flag, then to a starting tape (still utilized in steeplechasing) and from there to the use of starting stalls where a fair and even release is guaranteed. Clay Puett was influential in introducing them into American racing. They were first used in 1939 and some expressed surprise at their success. Puett, though, never had any doubts: "No one believed at that time that you could lock up thoroughbreds. They were too highly strung. Trainers, owners, starters and jockeys said I was barking up the wrong tree, that starting gates would never work, but I knew horses. I grew up on horses. I was convinced it was possible to teach a horse to race out of a closed gate."

And of course the starting stalls required another innovation: the all-important draw to determine which horse should start from which stall.

The advent of cameras and hi-speed photography meant that races became recorded, thereby helping stewards' enquiries into any potential misconduct. It also meant that the result could be determined beyond reasonable doubt through photo finishes; a far cry from the old days when, in the event of a perceived dead heat, the horses would have to run again.

Above: *The all-important winning post. Electronic video and photography has added far greater certainty to the outcome of races.*

Left: *Photo finish! Viewed, ridden by Blake Shinn, edges ahead of Bauer, to win the 2008 Melbourne Cup. In the early days, results were decided by the naked eye and in the event of a perceived dead heat, some match races were run again.*

Radio and television also transformed the sport. In Australia, Arnold 'Ike' Treloar first broadcast an entire race on radio in 1924. In Britain, the Derby and Grand National were first broadcast on radio in 1927, five years later the Derby was televised to an invited audience in London, and by 1946 racing was broadcast to domestic receivers. In America, Native Dancer was horse racing's first star of the small screen, the diamond silks of his jockey easy to follow even on fuzzy, small black and white models. When the horse lost by a head in the Kentucky Derby in 1953, viewers were simultaneously disappointed yet increasingly hooked into the sport.

Consequently it was written in the *New York Times*, "Horse racing, that used to be called the sport of kings, is threatening to become the king of sports." Nowadays, billions watch the big events each year and there are channels specifically devoted to horse racing. The advent of the internet has further advanced the media revolution.

Below: *Native Dancer, after winning at Belmont Park in New York. This is 1952 and the horse was one that caught the imagination of the American public, now able to view his exploits – in black and white of course – via the new innovation of television.*

The involvement of women in the sport has gradually increased. It is easy to overlook that it was only in 1966 that they were licensed to train in England, and another few years before it became possible for them to race ride. Gradually they have scaled the barriers that prevented them from entering an undeniably masculine environment. Julie Krone's 1993 win in the Belmont Stakes in America underlined their progress, as did Sheila Laxon's feat in becoming the first woman trainer to win the Melbourne Cup in 2001.

Above: *The Belmont Stakes, 1993, and a dirt-splattered Julie Krone strikes another blow for females in a male-dominated world by her victory on Colonial Affair. In recent years, women have become increasingly involved in the echelons of horse racing, notably as jockeys and trainers.*

Amongst other worldwide innovations are the transportation of thoroughbreds in aircraft, evening racing under lights, all-weather racetracks and a greater consciousness about the safety of both horses and jockeys. Skullcaps and chest guards, for instance, are now de rigueur for race riders.

However, there is a difference between rules as they are written and their enforcement. Racing writer Roger Longrigg wrote that the "rules of racing are largely, and increasingly, standard throughout the world. Their enforcement varies considerably, concerning such things as medication and rough riding. Standardization ought to be as complete, as universally accepted, as in tennis. We shall not see this until we watch Flying Childers, Lexington and Sea-Bird contest the Prix du Styx on the turf of the Elysian Fields."

Above: *Racehorses are loaded into aluminium stalls in a large private cargo plane prior to a journey from America to England. The ability to transport equine talent around the globe has been pivotal in altering the nature of the sport.*

Left: *Racing under floodlights, another modern innovation. This is Nad al Sheba, Dubai, in the United Arab Emirates. The lights can add a dramatic feel to the racing, and evening meetings mean that the sport takes place at a time that can be more convenient for spectators.*

Certainly, for all the uniformity there are also some noteworthy variations, some of which are inconsequential, if charming. For instance, in Great Britain races are not called race one, race two, etc, as they are in most other locations. Instead, the race is referred to by its starting time (the 2.25p.m. race at Epsom, for instance), its position in the race card (e.g. 'third race' or 'last race') and its name.

Another difference lies in the culture of American racing and racegoing, which places importance and emphasis on the clock. Day-to-day training is often undertaken with stopwatch in hand, and during races split-times are captured and displayed at various checkpoints by photo-electronic timers. Those timings are analysed in depth and great store is placed on the figures. So true aficionados of the sport can recite verbatim, say, the split-times of Secretariat in his Kentucky Derby win in 1973. Other nations are less inclined towards these statistics, possibly because the races tend to be more tactical in nature.

Other differences, though, are more significant. Take gambling, for example. This is a pivotal feature of horse racing – they are heavily reliant on each other – but the accompanying rules and regulations differ greatly.

Below: *Bookmakers take bets at the 2008 Cox Plate at the Moonee Valley racecourse in 2008. The importance of the relationship between gambling and horse racing cannot be overestimated. There is a mutual dependency.*

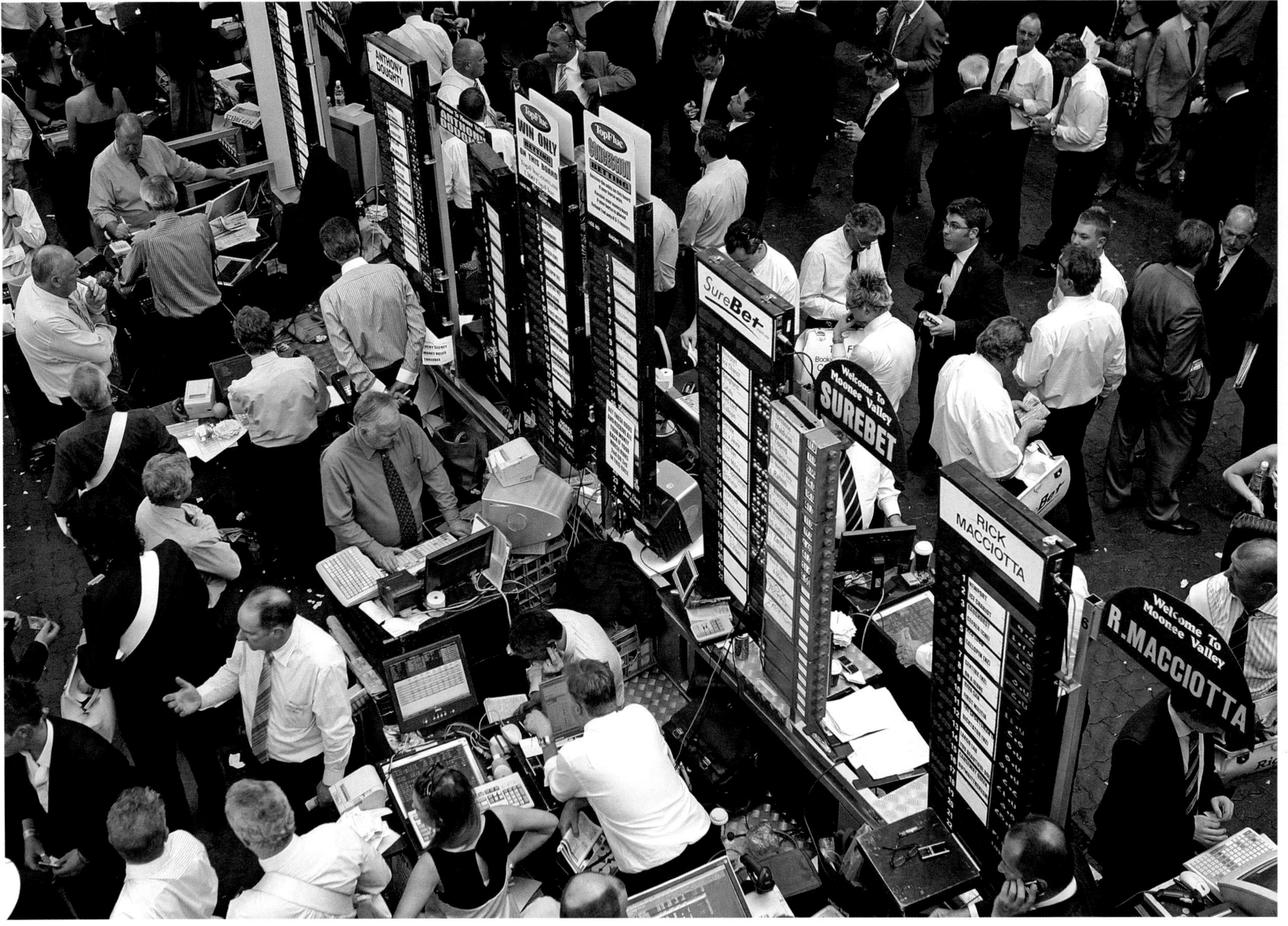

In America, betting is sanctioned and regulated by state governments, almost always through legalized pari-mutuel (tote) gambling stations. 'Pari-mutuel' is a French phrase which means 'betting amongst ourselves', where the gambled money is pooled and shared proportionally among the winners once a deduction is made from the pool. However, gambling is prohibited at some tracks, such as the Colonial Cup Steeplechase in Camden, South Carolina, because of a law passed in 1951.

Whilst pari-mutuel betting exists in all countries, the likes of Great Britain, Ireland and Australia also offer an alternative facility via independent bookmakers. In Great Britain and Ireland they operate both at the racecourse and off the course, whereas in Australia they only operate at the racecourse, where they compete with the tote.

Another significant difference in America is the legality of administering specific medications to thoroughbreds prior to competition. One is designed to stop them bleeding in the lungs, and then through the nostrils, during vigorous exercise. Another is a painkiller that helps to mask the discomfort that horses can feel when racing on the harsh, unforgiving dirt top surface that lies above a firm underlining base.

Above right: *The 2007 Breeders' Cup took place in quite abysmal weather. Conditions were labelled "sloppy" as the dirt turned to mud.*

Right: *The 2007 Breeders' Cup Classic. Curlin (number four) won in monsoon conditions. Races in America tend to take place on the "dirt", but abnormal weather like this affects all surfaces.*

These kind of surfaces are prevalent and encourage a flat-out dash from the stalls to the winning post. To support the desire for speed – and for consistency's sake – American racetracks are left-handed, one mile in distance, flat, and oval in shape.

However, the death of the filly Eight Belles, who broke down during the 2007 running of the Breeders' Cup, may accelerate the move to a more tolerant synthetic surface. The 2008 event in Santa Anita saw the use of the synthetic surface Pro-ride, which was well received but later removed. As yet there has been no major take-up of artificial track surfaces from manufacturers such as Fibretrack, Cushion Track and Polytrack, although Tapeta's synthetic surface was installed at the new Meydan Racecourse in Dubai.

Below: *Frankie Dettori rides Raven's Pass to the Breeders' Cup Classic at Santa Anita. The nature of the synthetic surface used at the racecourse – called Pro-ride – was felt by some to be more forgiving to the thoroughbreds.*

The blue riband events in Australia, Great Britain and Ireland are contested on turf, where the 'going' can be greatly impacted by weather conditions. In Britain and Ireland in particular no one course is like another and the differing shapes, sizes and undulations of the racetracks mean that each one has its own nuances. Newmarket and Epsom, for instance, are not even complete circuits.

American jockey Angel Cordero summarized the Euro-American differences: "The Europeans ride grass better than our jockeys. Here position is important. It's about speed. Over there, it's about finishing."

Steve Cauthen, another American, adds his thoughts on riding in Britain: "Of course there were a lot of things that were different. Most of all the tracks. One would be left-handed, another right, another straight, some downhill, some uphill, even a figure of eight. Your riders have been reared on them; I had to learn. And the pace of a race is much slower than at home, so I have made some adjustments, but a horse is still a horse."

That variety is the product of four centuries and more of history and heritage, and what is remarkable is that the 'green plots' at Newmarket, Epsom and Ascot that were uncovered by the likes of James I and Queen Anne have remained racing hotbeds through to the twenty-first century.

The modern Newmarket is a town where the stars are three thousand thoroughbreds, preened and pampered by a supporting cast of owners, trainers, stable lads and farriers. Nearly seventy per cent of the town's working population works in the racing industry, and of course, it can boast two top quality racecourses.

Epsom is still as quirky as it was two hundred years ago. People no longer flock there because of the medicinal qualities of the water, but come Derby Day it is not short of visitors. Up to one hundred thousand make the pilgrimage to view a remarkable sporting spectacle.

Midsummer in England still means Royal Ascot, as much a social occasion as a race meeting, forming part of a busy social calendar that includes the Henley Royal Regatta and tennis at Wimbledon. There is something timeless and very English about it all. In 1825 George IV instituted the tradition of the carriage procession of royalty down the racetrack in open landau carriages before racing each day – and the tradition remains. The current royal family attends every meeting, and has arrived in this manner each raceday since the Second World War – and what racing they have to feast their eyes upon, with several days of the highest class competition that Europe can offer.

Left: *The "sport of kings". Horse racing has been linked to royalty from its beginnings through to the twenty-first century. Queen Elizabeth II and Prince Philip, Duke of Edinburgh, arrive, as usual, by carriage at Royal Ascot in 2008.*

However, racing in Britain is not just about the blue riband events and the elite venues. There are nearly sixty racecourses dotted around the island, hosting around six million racegoers each year. Nowadays they can attend from January to December thanks to the introduction of all-weather tracks. The racing here is perhaps lower in quality and lower in profile but it helps to keep some of the five hundred professional jockeys in all-year employment.

Certainly, the nature of racing here has changed. Whilst there is still room for old-school trainers of the proven quality of Sir Michael Stoute, the ever increasing development of financially well-endowed operations such as Godolphin and Coolmore threatens to create something of a monopoly in breeding and purchasing the finest thoroughbred talent.

Godolphin's Saeed bin Suroor won the trainers' title in 1996, 1998, 1999 and 2004 and Aidan O'Brien (who won in 2001, 2002, 2007 and 2008) has enjoyed the fruits of Coolmore's slick operation with a conveyor belt of classic and group one victories both in England and in Ireland, where Leopardstown and the Curragh host the big racedays.

Certainly Coolmore helps to ensure that the Irish continue to exert influence in British racing, through their studs, their trainers and their vast array of ebullient racegoers who so love the 'craic' of big racedays.

Irish jockeys, too, are well-known. Mick Kinane and Johnny Murtagh have won globally as has perhaps the most talented of them all, Kieren Fallon (champion jockey in Britain in 1997, 1998, 1999, 2001, 2002 and 2003), whose radiant career has been clouded by controversy and allegations of corruption.

One who has never been accused of misdeeds, just an insatiable obsession with winning is Northern Ireland's jump jockey, Tony McCoy. A predecessor as champion, John Francome, sums up McCoy: "He is quite outstanding, the best jockey I have ever seen, since the days of my career in the saddle or since I retired." At this stage it is unknown whether McCoy will ultimately move into training, but history suggests that he may well do so. When jump racing is in the blood, beware the vice-like grip.

And if he does, he will no doubt hope that he trains an Irish horse that can follow in the hoof prints of Dawn Run, Arkle or the most recent wonder horse, multiple Gold Cup winner Best Mate. Certainly steeplechasing in Britain and Ireland remains prosperous and there is more informal 'point to point' racing for amateur riders.

Steeplechasing is also enjoyed in France but their race with the largest international following – suitably enticed by cosmic amounts of prize money – is the Prix de l'Arc de Triomphe, held at Longchamp on the first Sunday in October. It provides a celebrated finale to the European season in the majestic surroundings of the Bois de Boulogne. Each new year seems to bring new theatre, and it often provides a fitting climax to an illustrious equine career. It is not just Europeans who consider it to be the most significant event in the turf's global calendar.

Above: *Northern Ireland's Tony McCoy. Probably the best jump jockey of the modern era. Driven, courageous and a skilled race rider.*

Right: *A blue riband day in the racing calendar. Europe's celebrated finale to each season takes place in the grandeur and crackling atmosphere of Longchamp for the Prix de l'Arc de Triomphe.*

18
LONGCHAMP

Right: *Frankie Dettori breaks his Epsom Derby duck on Authorized in 2007. The Italian-born jockey has become one of the most popular and best known racing personalities.*

Below: *Damien Oliver and Falvelon move at speed on their way to victory on the Schillaci Stakes at Caulfield in Melbourne. Both horse and jockey have been prominent in Australia's growing impact within the sport.*

The other French classics are shared between Longchamp and Chantilly – and there are more than two hundred and fifty racecourses in the country, many of them appealingly located in the countryside. France has also become a major player in the bloodstock industry with locally bred thoroughbreds making their mark, both 'on the flat' and 'over the sticks'.

Italy has a tenth of the racetracks of France but it can, of course, boast 'Fun-time Frankie' Dettori, the Milan-born jockey who has become one of the most famous sportsmen in Europe thanks to his high achievement and engaging personality. Dettori loves the camera and has done much to promote the sport, although his reputation was somewhat tarnished by a six-month ban for a failed drugs test in 2012, shortly after which Godolphin announced they would not be renewing his retainer in 2013. Dettori had suffered the frustration of not winning the Epsom Derby, but he put that right in 2007 with victory on board Authorized.

Germany, the Czech Republic and Turkey are other European countries where racing is popular. However, in the modern era, perhaps the heart of racing beats most vigorously in Australia.

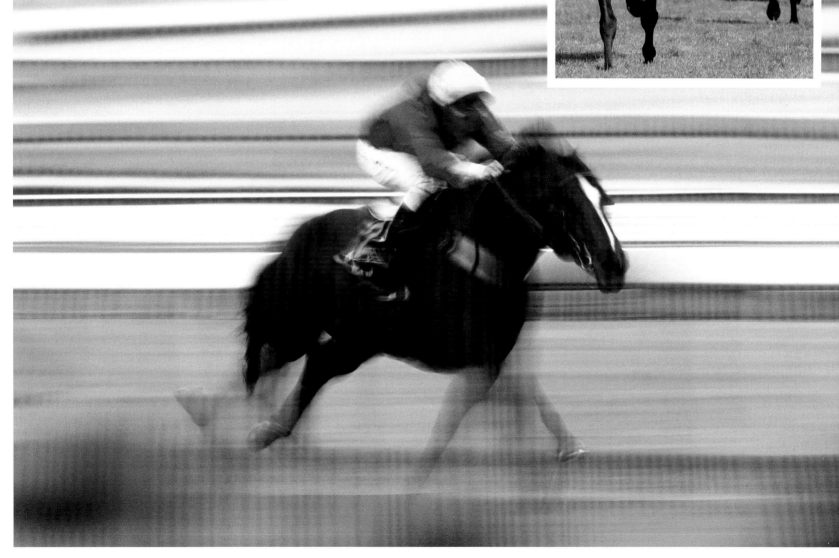

It has become one of the major racing nations for a variety of reasons. Firstly, its breeding operations (many shuttle sires visit here) are numerous and productive. Australia has produced some star-studded thoroughbreds recently. Northerly and Falvelon, both foaled in 1996, are two such examples.

Northerly was known as the 'fighting tiger' and won two Cox Plates, two Australian Cups and a Caulfield Cup. Sports journalist Les Carlyon summed up: "He fools you every time he races. He has the body language of a loser and a heart as big as Nullarbor. He invariably looks to be struggling, a shambles of a horse blundering around on memory while his jockey pumps and blusters. Then he gets going. One instant Northerly looks beaten, the next he looks unbeatable. The closer he gets to the post, the harder he tries. He grinds on. And on. He simply refuses to be beaten."

The bay, Falvelon was the Australian Champion Sprinter in 2001–2 and 2002–3 and has gone on to become a big success at stud, ensuring the production line of Aussie thoroughbred talent rolls on.

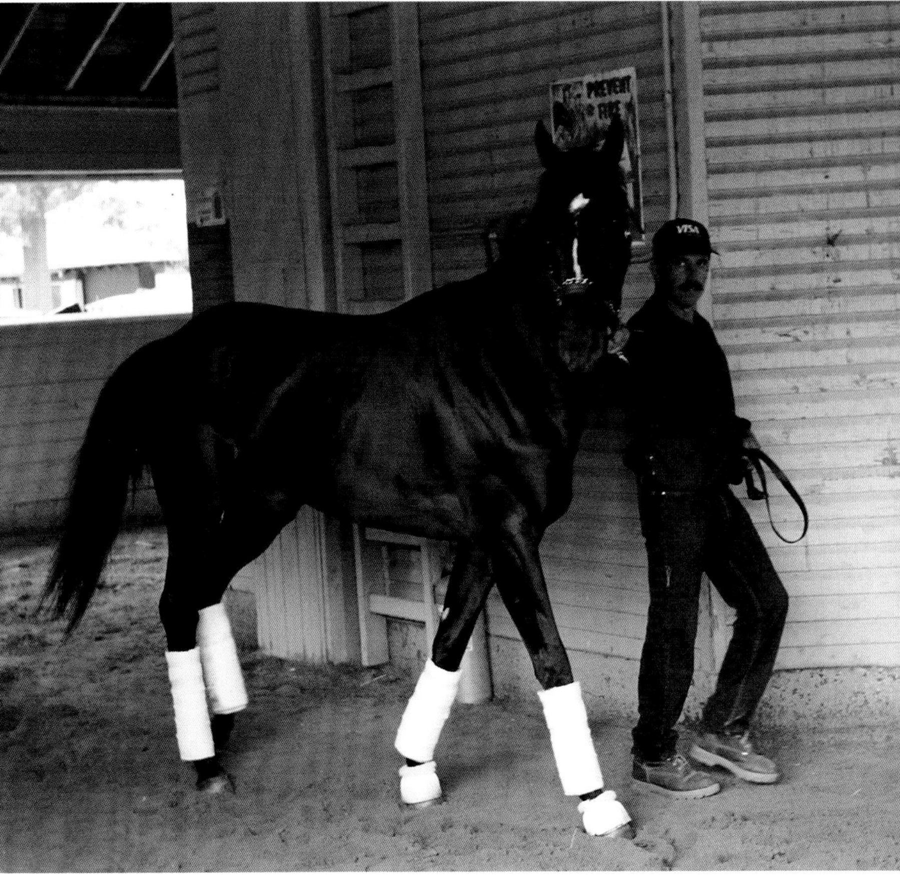

Above: *Near miss one. War Emblem won the Kentucky Derby and Preakness Stakes in 2002 but failed to secure the Triple Crown at Belmont.*

Left: *Darren Beadman – another top-quality Australian jockey – celebrates another win, this time on Valedictum during the 2008 Golden Slipper meeting at Rosehill racecourse in Sydney.*

There has also been a welcome stream of top race riders, notably Damien Oliver – who frequently rode Falvelon – and Darren Beadman, who quite apart from his illustrious record as a race rider – including Melbourne Cup triumphs on Kingston Rule in 1990 and Saintly in 1995 – is noteworthy because he retired in 1997 to enter the ministry with the Christian Life Centre at Waterloo, Australia, before returning three years later.

Certainly, the globalization of the sport at the end of the twentieth century was good for Australia and it continues to reap the benefits. Horse racing is its third most attended spectator sport behind Australian rules football and rugby league. It is estimated that around two million racegoers attend around three thousand race meetings at five hundred racecourses dotted around its vast expanses.

These include:

- Caulfield in Melbourne, home of the Caulfield Cup
- Sydney's Randwick and Rosehill, the latter host to the Golden Slipper
- Morphettville, Victoria Park and Cheltenham in Adelaide
- Brisbane's Eagle Farm and Doomben racetracks, who host the Stradbroke Handicap and the Doomben 10000 respectively.

But it is Flemington that is far and away the best known of the country's racing venues, primarily because its feature race, the Melbourne Cup, continues to capture the imagination.

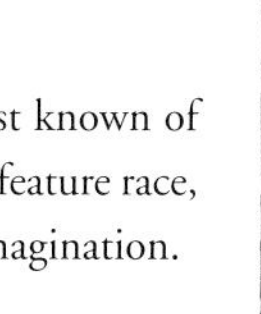

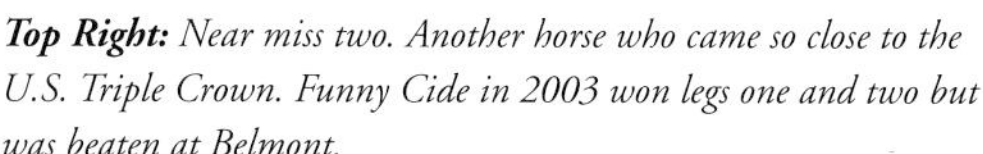

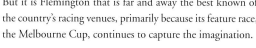

Top Right: *Near miss two. Another horse who came so close to the U.S. Triple Crown. Funny Cide in 2003 won legs one and two but was beaten at Belmont.*

Right: *Near miss three. Smarty Jones receives the hurrahs and plaudits after winning the Preakness Stakes in 2004. After enduring an eye injury during his development, it would have been an exciting story if Smarty Jones could have won the Triple Crown. But, for the third year running, a horse fell just short of making history.*

This is a sporting spectacle that Melbourne, indeed the whole of Australia, is proud to host. They intuitively view the race as an opportunity to showcase their nation. So it was publicity when, in 2003, 2004 and 2005, the mare, Makybe Diva, became the first to win it three times.

Perhaps it is a surprise that there have not been equivalents of Makybe Diva in the United States of America in the early part of the new millennium. Five aspirants, War Emblem (2002), Funny Cide (2003), Smarty Jones (2004), Big Brown (2008) and I'll Have Another (2012) won the Kentucky Derby and the Preakness Stakes to give themselves an opportunity to emulate Secretariat, Seattle Slew and Affirmed in the 1970s and achieve a Triple Crown.

However, in the final leg at Belmont, War Emblem tripped at the start, Funny Cide was outpaced, and Big Brown finished last. I'll Have Another was withdrawn due to tendonitis on the eve of the race and was retired.

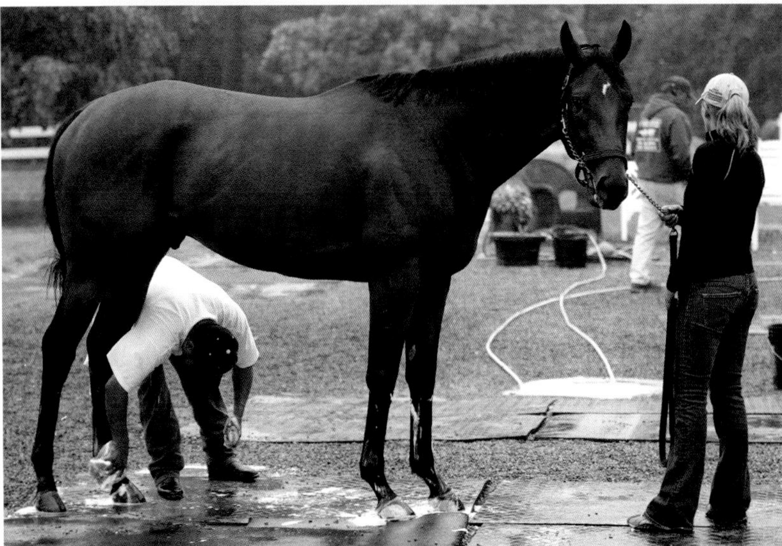

Left: *Near miss four. Big Brown gets washed before the Belmont Stakes in 2008. Yet again a prime contender for the U.S. Triple Crown came up short at the end. In fact, Big Brown finished last, drained of spark and energy.*

Below: *Sunline and her first foal – suitably spindle-legged and uncoordinated – at Cambridge Stud, New Zealand. Another success for the New Zealand bloodstock industry.*

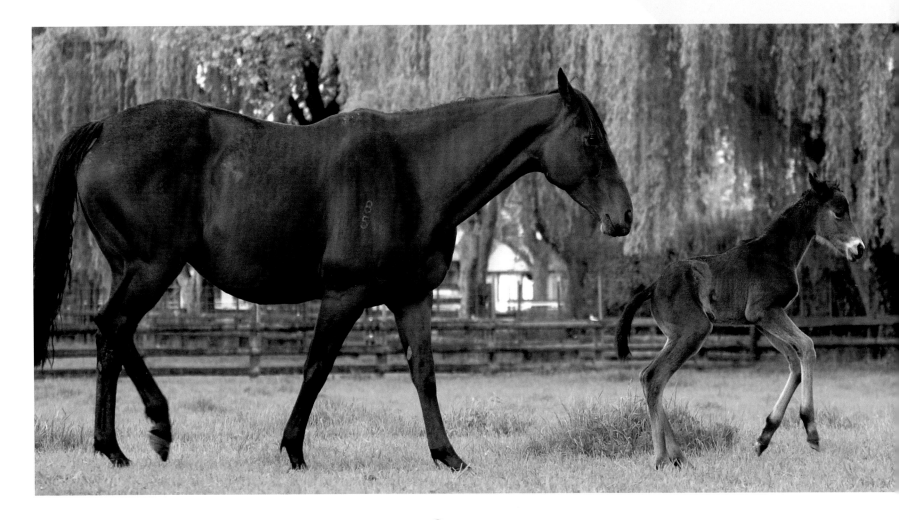

***Right:** Sunline in her racing days, winning at Flemington racecourse in 2001 to secure the Four 'n' Twenty Turnbull Stakes.*

The horse that got closest to the much-vaunted 'triple' was Philadelphia's Smarty Jones, whose story had endeared him to racegoers. He had fractured his skull and shattered the orbital bones around his left eye on a starting gate before he had even raced. Nevertheless, when he won the second leg of the triple by eleven and a half lengths at Pimlico, he evoked memories of Secretariat and there were more than one hundred and twenty thousand at Belmont, the biggest sports gathering ever in New York, to see if history would be made.

For a while it looked like they would be rewarded. "The whip is out on Smarty Jones! It's been twenty-six years! One furlong away!" exclaimed racecourse commentator Tom Durkin as they came into sight of the winning post. But Durkin was premature. Outsider Birdstone won by a length.

No matter, with more than sixty million racegoers a year, horse racing is making a good fist of competing against alternative attractions such as American football and basketball. The high point of the season has traditionally been the Kentucky Derby but with every passing year that comparative newcomer, the Breeders' Cup, comes increasingly to the fore. The 2008 event was held over two days (the first for fillies and mares, the second for colts) at Santa Anita on the edge of Los Angeles and culminated in the five million U.S. dollars Breeders' Classic.

***Right:** A colourful and attractive scene at the Ellerslie racecourse in Auckland, New Zealand, on Boxing Day, 2007. Nowadays, at almost any time, horse racing is taking place somewhere on the planet.*

Right: *The great Makybe Diva, ridden by Glen Boss (blue colours in centre), on her way to winning the 2004 Melbourne Cup. She won three times in a row, creating further welcome publicity for Australia's blue riband horse racing event. Australia simply grinds to a standstill on raceday.*

Incidentally, thoroughbred racing is not the only form of racing in the country. Harness racing and quarter horse racing also have their fans. 'Quarter horses' are even fleeter of foot than thoroughbreds, though they run over shorter distances. While a thoroughbred race ranges from five furlongs to one and a half miles, the average quarter horse equivalent is about a quarter of a mile, hence the name. Quarter horses, of course, are short and muscular, constructed for speed and speed alone. The races are devoid of turns and tactics but photo finishes are the norm.

Racing with specific breeds – such as Arabian – also takes place in North America as does harness racing ('standardbred'). Indeed Canada's main racing venue, Toronto's Woodbine racetrack, stages both thoroughbred and harness racing on the same day. It was also the venue for the 1996 Breeders' Cup, which emphasized the strong American–Canadian links. That said, Canada has a Triple Crown all of its own – the Queen's Plate (first run in 1860), Prince of Wales's Stakes and the Breeders' Stakes – as well as a strong breeding culture. Northern Dancer and Nijinsky are the most obvious examples of Canadian-born talent.

That North American connection mirrors that of Australia and New Zealand, for the Kiwi bloodstock industry has been effective in producing thoroughbreds that thrive in Australia (as well as Asia). Most obvious is the legendary Phar Lap. But in the 1970s Think Big did a Melbourne Cup double and more recently Might and Power and Sunline were also hugely successful.

Left: *A horse pool at the San Isidro racetrack. Of course, the preparation, recovery and recuperation of thoroughbreds have become more scientific and hi-tec down the years.*

Think Big was foaled in 1970 and was purchased by popular Australian Bart Cummings at the Trentham yearling sales in New Zealand for a Malaysian businessman, Dato Tan Chin Nam. Cummings, a Melbourne Cup specialist, then trained him to success at Flemington in 1974 and again – having not won since and at odds of thirty-three to one – in 1975.

The versatile Might and Power won the Melbourne Cup twenty-two years later, following success in the Caulfield Cup. A year later he added the Doomben Cup and the Cox Plate amongst others.

Sunline, two years older, won thirty out of forty-eight races in Australia, New Zealand and Hong Kong. Of mares, only Makybe Diva has won more prize money, and Sunline was Horse of the Year three times in a row in Australia and four times in a row in New Zealand.

New Zealand racing goes back to colonial times and its sixty racecourses attract more than a million racegoers. The race of the year, the New Zealand Derby, is run in Auckland on Boxing Day.

Europe, North America, Australasia – all are continents where horse racing is well established, but there are also a number of countries outside these areas with a proud racing past and a thriving present.

***Left:** Admire Moon, ridden by Yasunari Iwata, wins the 2007 Japan Cup in great style at the Tokyo racecourse.*

South Africa – where the first recorded race club meeting took place in 1802, and nowadays fifty thousand attend the Durban July Handicap at Greville racecourse each year, with betting running into the hundreds of millions of rands.

Mauritius – where as long ago as 1812 the Mauritius Turf Club, the second oldest racecourse in the world, was founded by Colonel Draper.

Argentina – the principal racing nation in South America, with long-established racecourses in Buenos Aires.

Hong Kong – where the British influence is still felt and the Royal Hong Kong Jockey Club conducts nearly seven hundred races every season at the Happy Valley and Sha Tin racetracks. The sport contributes more than ten per cent of Hong Kong's tax revenue via gambling.

Japan – with twenty thousand horse races a year – flat racing, jump racing (hurdles), and Ban'ei racing (also called draft racing) across thirty racetracks. Not to mention jockeys of the quality of Yutaka Take, a national icon.

Above: *Yutaka Take riding Admire Moon returns to the unsaddling area after the 2007 Audemars Piguet Queen Elizabeth II Cup at the Sha Tin racecourse in Hong Kong. Note the vast crowds in the background.*

Left: *A firework flash of colour illuminates a dark night sky in Dubai. A remarkable scene at the Nad al Sheba racecourse prior to the 2008 running of the Dubai World Cup. Horse racing is part of the entertainment industry and finds innovative ways to boost its popularity.*

Dubai – that comparatively new kid on the racing block, but now hugely influential, thanks to the work of Sheikh Mohammed and the Godolphin operation. In many ways the flavour, style and prosperity of the Dubai World Cup symbolizes the new order at the upper end of horse racing. Watching top-class thoroughbreds racing under the lights on the fringes of the desert is a not-to-be-forgotten experience, as is the week of festivities that prefaces it.

Yet perhaps horse racing is not so different now from when, in 1744, England's *Westminster Journal* reported of a match race at Lincoln, "There was a very extraordinary horse race between a six-year-old horse and one aged twenty-one. They ran fourteen miles round the said course and performed it in thirty-nine minutes for one hundred guineas – which were won by the former by only a horse's length. There were great wagers laid and the greatest concourse of people ever seen there."

So much has changed down the years, yet so much remains the same. The pastime of watching horses in competition is still about the sense of occasion, the thrill of the contest – perhaps spiced by a gamble – and the seemingly unshakable connection between the human and equine species. And long may it continue.

Below: *High fashion on Ladies' Day at Royal Ascot in England, 2008. At many events, racegoers enjoy the social aspect and camaraderie of the sport every bit as much as the actual racing.*

Index

Acknowledgements

The Publisher and author would like to thank the following people and organizations for their kind help and contribution:

Page 19 top left: Courtesy of the Maryland Jockey Club.

Page 96: Mark Cranham.

Getty Images.

Topfoto.

Library of Congress USA.

Amanda Thomas at Wolverhampton Race Course.

Thanks to Timothy Cox and his vast library of horse racing books.

Special photography courtesy of Mirco De Cet.

Bibliography

A Concise History of British Horse Racing. Hilary Bracegirdle, English Life Publications, 1999 (created for the national horse racing museum).

Classic Horse Races. Anne Holland, Macdonald and Co, 1989.

Classic Horse-racing Quotes. Graham Sharpe, Robson Books, 2005.

Complete A-Z of Horse Racing. Sean Magee, Channel 4 Books, 2001.

Derby 200. Michael Seth-Smith, Roger Mortimer, Guinness Superlatives Limited, 1979.

Frank Keating's Sporting Century. Frank Keating, Robson Books, 1997.

Front Runners. Brough Scott, Victor Gollancz Ltd, 1991.

Horse Racing's Top 100 Moments. By the staff of Blood-Horse Publications, Eclipse Press, 2006.

Horse Sense: An Inside Look at the Sport of Kings. Bert Sugar with Cornell Richardson, John Wiley and Sons Inc, 2003.

Newmarket: From James I to the Present Day. Laura Thompson, Virgin, 2000.

The Complete Encyclopedia of Horse Racing. Bill Mooney and George Ennor, Carlton Books, 2007.

The Racing Tribe: Watching the Horsewatchers. Kate Fox, Metro Publishing, 2005.

The World of Horse Racing. Brough Scott and Gerry Cranham, Gallery Books, 1987.

1000 Racing Quotations. Graham Sharpe, Highdown, 2007.